Gambling

Gambling laws are to face their biggest shakeup in 30 years, under government blueprints for reform. Simon Jeffery explains

What will happen?
US-style casinos and gambling resorts, such as Las Vegas, could soon become part of Britain's leisure industry, if parliament scraps many of the betting restrictions in the 1968 Gaming Act.

Who is suggesting this?
The former chief economic adviser to the Treasury, Sir Alan Budd, who has prepared a report for the government on the liberalisation of the gaming industry. The Home Office originally commissioned it in 1999 but it has since been taken over by the Department of Culture, Media and Sport.

Which parts of the 1968 Act will go?
The report proposes to do away with the following regulations:
- No live music
- No more than 10 slot machines in casinos (two in betting shops)
- A maximum jackpot of £15 from slot machines
- No warm food in betting shops
- No drinks at gaming tables
- No non-members admitted to casinos
- The 24-hour 'cooling off period' between joining a casino and being allowed to enter
- No more than one betting shop within a 400m radius

What difference will it make?
The proposals will make visiting casinos and betting shops a more pleasant experience, equivalent perhaps to restaurants and nightclubs. Live entertainment will entice customers who want to do more than play with their money, and scrapping the membership requirements will allow less than committed gamblers to attend.

By Simon Jeffery

British casinos could become much like those in Las Vegas and Atlantic City, allowing bingo, betting and games under one roof.

Why is the present law so restrictive?
The intention was to keep criminals out of gambling and clean up the scandal-hit casinos. However, the UK gaming industry now has a good reputation, despite a number of high-profile cases at the end of the 1970s when a number of licences were revoked.

Does liberalisation mean more people will gamble?
The report proposes a ban on fruit machines in fish and chip shops and cafés (to curb the chances of under-18 gambling) but churches and charities worry there will be a growth in addiction. Little is known about the social impact of deregulated gaming. In Australia, it created greater problem-gambling and a consumer backlash.

What about the lottery?
It was introduced in 1994 and – despite some early fears – has not created widespread gambling addiction. A 1998 survey by GamCare, a group which studies the impact of gambling, found that 65% of the population had played the national lottery in the previous year – just under the 72% who took part in some form of gambling activity. This is below the nine in 10 adults in Sweden and New Zealand who gambled over the same period.

How prevalent is problem-gambling?
The GamCare survey found that 0.8% of British gamblers could be classified as 'problem'; lower than the United States (1.1%), Australia

(2.3%) and Spain (1.4%). But this figure may rise with deregulation.

Who will benefit?
If gambling laws are relaxed, casino operators can expect to see a big boost in profits as they expand into new markets. This may have a knock-on effect for certain towns: Blackpool has already unveiled ambitious plans to turn itself into the Las Vegas of the north, and proposals for the first of five hotels, featuring 1,000 bedrooms, 3,000 slot machines and 80 gaming tables, have already been drawn up. Some see it as a boost for the north-west and for British tourism in general.

Why has no one suggested it before?
The gaming laws were last reviewed in 1996, when casinos and bingo halls were allowed to advertise for the first time. Moves were also made to set up casinos in certain towns where they were banned.

A safe bet?

Information from GamCare

Gambling – a safe bet?
Most young people in the UK gamble. It's become part of our lifestyle. We all take risks, and gambling is a kind of risk taking that's fun and exciting.

Have you ever daydreamed about 'the big win' – winning a million on the Lottery, a few thousand on scratchcards or the jackpot on the slot machines? This fantasy of winning encourages us to take part. And if we win, or nearly win, we're tempted to carry on gambling.

Gambling makes you feel good, but it can be harmful. Some types of gambling are very habit forming, like scratchcards, fruit machines or playing cards or pool for money with friends or colleagues. The urge to gamble can take over and become an addiction that can destroy the gambler and their family. And an addiction to gambling can be just as damaging as drug or alcohol dependency.

Who really wins?
The chances are it won't be you! A few gamblers win it big but most lose overall. The real winners are the gambling industry, who turnover around £115 million every day, and the Government, who take over £1.5 billion in gambling tax per year!

What are the odds of winning?
These are some of the (approximate) odds of winning:

National Lottery	14,000,000 to 1
Slot machines	600 to 1
Roulette	36 to 1
Scratchcards	5.5 to 1

Keep it under control
Gambling can quickly get out of control and create serious problems in your life. So, when you gamble, remember:

- You're buying fun, not investing your money
- Before playing, set strict limits on how much time and money you're going to spend
- Quit while you're ahead
- Only gamble with money you can afford to lose
- Don't 'chase' your losses
- Keep up other interests and hobbies – don't let gambling take over
- Gambling in moderation is okay and healthy
- The key is … gamble responsibly!

What about me – have I got a problem?
If you or other people are worried that you may be gambling too much, think about the following questions:

- Have I ever lied about my gambling, or lied to get money for gambling?
- Do I spend more than I can afford on gambling?
- When I lose money, do I want to gamble some more to win back my losses?
- Do I gamble because I can't handle stress or worries in my life?
- Do I think about gambling when I should be concentrating on other things?
- Have I ever skipped school, college or work to gamble?

If you answer 'yes' to any of these questions, your gambling may be taking over your life, and you need to get further advice. Phone the confidential GamCare helpline 0845 6000 133. At the other end of the phone will be someone who knows what you're going through and isn't going to judge you. They can give you real help and advice.

• The above information is from a leaflet produced and published by GamCare, see page 41 for their address details.

What can I gamble on?
There are lots of things you can legally gamble on in the UK. Each activity has its own set of rules for playing and almost all have a minimum age restriction:

*Slot machines/cash tokens**	Any age	*Lottery*	16
*£15 cash jackpot***	18	*Pools*	16
Horses	18	*Casinos*	18
Dogs	18	*Bingo*	18

* Many places that have fruit machines choose to have a minimum age for entry.

** These should be kept separate from other machines

There are severe penalties for any operator who allows under-age gambling.

Lottery gives women a taste for gambling

More and more women are gambling – because the National Lottery has made it socially acceptable.

Having a flutter is the fastest growing leisure activity outside the home, say researchers.

According to market research analysts Mintel, the lottery has created a demand for different forms of gambling from the traditional betting on horse racing.

Women are not keen on going into betting shops, but they feel comfortable about buying a National Lottery ticket or visiting a bingo hall.

However, having a flutter on a horse while enjoying a day at the races at such courses as Ascot, Cheltenham and Aintree is also increasingly popular with women.

Mintel said: 'Women are far less embarrassed at placing a bet at a race meeting than going into a betting shop, which still holds something of a stigma as far as they are concerned.'

The Mintel report shows that one in five adults place a bet at least once a week, while almost three-quarters admit to gambling at least once a year.

More than two out of three adults – 68 per cent – have bought a lottery ticket in the last six months, and the UK game remains the most successful state-run lottery in Europe.

The bingo is enjoying a revival. The number of clubs declined by 15 per cent as the lottery gained popularity after its launch in 1994, but admissions to clubs now exceed the 100 million recorded in 1995.

> **'Women are far less embarrassed at placing a bet at a race meeting than going into a betting shop, which still holds something of a stigma as far as they are concerned'**

The main casualty of the lottery's success has been the football pools. The survey shows that only 8 per cent of adults have participated in the pools in the last six months.

Around a quarter of UK adults have placed a bet either with a bookmaker or on a racetrack in the last six months with men twice as likely as women to go into a bookmaker's shop.

Mintel says betting shops have invested substantially in new interiors and features but this has done little to transform the downmarket image of the shops.

Well-off people are not attracted to betting shops, with adults in the lower income groups twice as likely to visit. In fact 40 per cent of the better-off do not even know where their nearest betting shop is, and the report says considerable efforts will be needed to capture this market.

Nearly half of punters place bets under £5 in value when they gamble in betting shops, at a horse or dog race, over the phone or the Internet. Only 5 per cent admit to exceeding £30 on their bet.

The Mintel report predicts a 21 per cent increase in expenditure on gambling between 1999 and 2004.

The rise in gambling in Britain was highlighted last week in a BBC documentary.

The programme, *Jackpot*, which examined various types of gambling, followed three bingo fans who play each week at the Mecca Forge in Glasgow.

© The Daily Mail
August, 2001

Lottery guide

Information from the National Lottery Commission

National Lottery games

The National Lottery was introduced in 1994 to raise money for the Good Causes. It currently comprises three types of games:

- The National Lottery Game – the twice weekly draw.
- Thunderball™ – weekly draw.
- Lottery Extra – twice weekly draw
- National Lottery Instants™ – scratchcard games.

Who's who?

The players

- 82% of households have played the National Lottery draw game since its launch in November 1994.
- In an independent survey published by the National Lottery Commission in May 1999, 71% of households reported playing the main National Lottery draw game in the previous week and 32% reported playing in both the Wednesday and Saturday draw. Households that played only on a Saturday were found to spend, on average, £2.49, and those that play twice each week, on average £5.37.
- In a typical week, about 6% of the population will buy a National Lottery Instants™. The average amount spent is £2.64.
- Anyone 16 and over can play the on-line games and Instants™ games, but it is a criminal offence for retailers or Camelot to sell tickets to younger people. Under-16s are not entitled to any prize money, and Camelot is entitled to reclaim any prize money paid against tickets bought by under-16s.
- Players have to buy tickets in the United Kingdom or the Isle of Man, where tickets first went on sale in December 1999. An exception to this is made for British forces abroad. Most countries prohibit the import of foreign lottery tickets and

NATIONAL LOTTERY COMMISSION

Camelot does not sell its tickets abroad, even by subscription. Tickets bought in this country and resold abroad are invalid.

Camelot Group plc – the operator of the National Lottery

The National Lottery is operated by Camelot Group plc, a private sector company owned by a consortium of other companies: Racal Electronics plc, Cadbury Schweppes plc, International Computers Ltd and De La Rue plc. OFLOT originally awarded Camelot the licence to run the National Lottery in 1994 following a competitive application process in which Camelot offered to run the National Lottery keeping less for its costs and profit and giving more to Good Causes than any other bidder. Camelot successfully bid to run the National Lottery for another seven years in another competitive bidding process last year.

The game promoters

Although Camelot has a 7-year licence to operate the National Lottery, each game needs a separate promoter's licence. All current games are provided by Camelot, although Vernons Lotteries Ltd promoted Easy Play™ from August 1998 to May 1999.

Retailers

To ensure that tickets are readily accessible, over 35,000 retailers including corner shops, petrol stations, post offices and supermarkets, sell National Lottery tickets. Over 24,000 of these have a National Lottery 'On-line' terminal linked by secure circuits to Camelot's computers. These retailers sell tickets and pay prizes for both the on-line games and the Instants™ games. Close to a further 11,000 have simpler terminals and sell tickets and pay prizes for the Instants™ games only. National Lottery retailers are required to comply with strict rules, which include requirements to provide lottery information to players, and a requirement not to sell tickets to under-16s.

The National Lottery Commission

The National Lottery Commission replaced the Director General and his office – OFLOT – on 1 April 1999. The Government decided that a National Lottery Commission

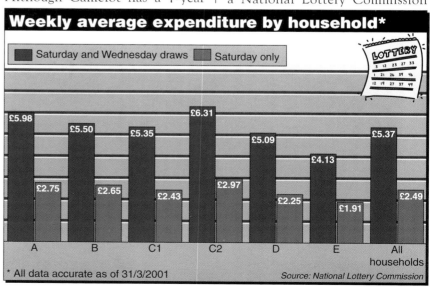

Weekly average expenditure by household*

Saturday and Wednesday draws | Saturday only

	Saturday and Wednesday draws	Saturday only
A	£5.98	£2.75
B	£5.50	£2.65
C1	£5.35	£2.43
C2	£6.31	£2.97
D	£5.09	£2.25
E	£4.13	£1.91
All households	£5.37	£2.49

* All data accurate as of 31/3/2001

Source: National Lottery Commission

should replace the post of Director General as the regulator of the lottery to ensure that in future there was less risk, actual or perceived, of conflicts of interest and that a wider range of knowledge, experience and expertise could be brought to bear on the regulation of the lottery.

The National Lottery Commission comprises five members who are appointed by the Secretary of State for Culture, Media and Sport. The current commissioners are: Lord (Terence) Burns, Brian Pomeroy, Harriet Spicer, Rosalind Gilmore and Timothy Hornsby. Lord Burns currently holds the position of Chairman. The appointment as Chair can be for no longer than twelve months but a Commissioner can be reappointed as Chair after a period equal to that of their appointment has expired.

The National Lottery Commission has three statutory duties under the National Lottery etc. Act 1993:

- To ensure that the National Lottery is run with all due propriety
- To protect the interests of players and provided that these first two objectives are met
- To maximise the money raised for the Good Causes.

The National Lottery Commission, like other Non Departmental Public Bodies, is funded by grant in aid. This is provided by the Department for Culture, Media and Sport from monies provided to the department by Parliament. The grant is recoverable from the National Lottery Distribution Fund and licence fees.

National Lottery Distribution Fund (NLDF)

The fund, which is administered by the Department for Culture, Media and Sport, receives money from Camelot every Tuesday in respect of tickets sold in the previous week. The money is invested by the National Debt Commissioners for the benefit of the NLDF. The distribution of the fund is the job of the distributing organisations (see below).

When an award has been made by one of the distributing bodies

---

The National Lottery so far

- February 1994 – Eight bids to run the National Lottery were received by OFLOT.
- May 1994 – Camelot was selected to run the National Lottery.
- 19 November 1994 – The first draw was held.
- 21 March 1995 – Instants™ went on sale.
- 5 February 1997 – The first Wednesday draw was held.
- 11 April 1998 – Contributions to Good Causes reached £5 billion.
- 10 August 1998 – Easy Play™ was launched.
- 1 April 1999 – The National Lottery Commission replaces OFLOT.
- 7 June 1999 – Thunderball™ was launched.
- 13 November 2000 – Lottery Extra™ was launched.

(responsible for assessing grants) the NLDF is responsible for releasing the appropriate funds.

The distributing organisations

There are 13 organisations that decide who should receive a National Lottery award. These are named below and the percentage of funds they receive from the NLDF is shown in brackets:

- The Sports and Arts Councils of England, Scotland, Wales and Northern Ireland (16.66% each).
- The Heritage Lottery Fund, which provides funds to preserve, restore or acquire the heritage that makes up the fabric of our history and culture. The item must have some special local, regional or national importance to the heritage (16.66%).
- The National Lottery Charities Board, which allocates funds to help those who are disadvantaged and other institutions established for charitable purposes (16.66%).
- The New Opportunities Fund which allocates grants for expenditure on health, education and the environment (13.33%). The

Secretary of State may order that some of the funds allocated to the New Opportunities Fund be given to the National Endowment for Science, Technology and the Arts (NESTA).

Each distributing organisation is independent of Government but has to follow guidelines, established by the Secretary of State for Culture, Media and Sport, when deciding who should receive National Lottery money.

The integrity of the draw

Extensive steps are taken to safeguard the integrity of the draw. Some of these measures are listed below:

- The equipment (including ball sets) used in the National Lottery draws is subject to regular independent testing. The testing process is, in turn, monitored by the National Lottery Commission.
- All draws are undertaken in accordance with procedures approved by the National Lottery Commission and in the presence of an independent auditor. Furthermore, the Commission itself has a presence at two draws each month.
- All draw equipment is stored to the highest security standards between draws. For example, arrangements are in place to ensure that no draw machine or ball set may be accessed except in the presence of an independent auditor.
- Given the above, the identity of the actual draw machine and ball set selected for use at any one draw is irrelevant to the outcome of that draw.
- The outcome of the draws is regularly monitored for randomness by both Camelot and the National Lottery Commission. The Commission's assurance of randomness is commissioned through the Royal Statistical Society.

- The above information is an extract from the National Lottery Commission's Lottery Guide which is available on their web site: www.natlotcomm.gov.uk

© National Lottery Commission

Where does the money go?

Information from the National Lottery Commission

The money spent by players on lottery tickets is shared out amongst the following stake-holders:

- Prize winners – 50%
- The National Lottery Distribution Fund (for the Good Causes) – 28%
- The Treasury (through Lottery Duty) – 12%
- Retailers – 5%
- Camelot (and its shareholders and suppliers) – 5%

The proportions given above are approximate. The actual shares depend on a number of factors. These are designed to maximise the benefit to Good Causes and ensure a fair deal for other stakeholders. For example:

- As sales rise, Camelot's percentage share reduces and the NLDF's share increases. Consequently it is not possible to calculate exactly what percentage of the money will be kept by Camelot and by the NLDF until the actual level of sales is known.
- Slightly different figures apply to each year, even if sales remain constant. In the early years the share to Camelot was slightly higher to take account of their initial capital outlay.
- The formula for calculating the percentages to be shared between Camelot and the NLDF is subject to adjustment for inflation so that it preserves the value to the NLDF.
- Any prize money that winners fail to claim must be passed to the NLDF after 180 days.
- Any other money earmarked to be offered as prize money that is not paid as prizes must be handed to the NLDF (this money is known as the 'Prize Target Shortfall' and is explained later in this article).

The value of prizes in each game

The value of prizes in the different

NATIONAL LOTTERY COMMISSION

games can vary widely. The rules of the draw game, for example, state that Camelot will use 45% of the money taken in ticket sales for each draw to form the Prize Fund for that draw – though from time to time Camelot is allowed to add extra money in the form of Superdraws. The prizes paid for Thunderball™ are fixed and range from £5 to £250,000. The value of prizes within each Instants™ game also varies: the value of prizes in any Instants™ game, measured as a percentage of the face value of the tickets, has so far ranged from about 55% to 65%.

The National Lottery Commission requires Camelot to display in every National Lottery retailer detailed information about the value of prizes and other aspects of each game to help people make informed decisions about which games to play. This information is also made available through the National Lottery Line.

Prize target shortfall

Because prize percentages in different games vary, the actual total percentage pay-out across the whole portfolio of National Lottery games depends on the numbers of tickets that players choose to buy for various games. The licence sets a target of 50% pay-out for the National Lottery as a whole. If the actual pay-out is less, the balance (known as the 'Prize Target Shortfall') goes to benefit the Good Causes.

Other revenue for the NLDF

Prize money is held in a secure trust fund on behalf of winners. Interest earned by this fund passes to the NLDF, as does interest earned on any money earmarked to fund prizes but not used for this purpose. Any profits generated by the sale of goods, such as National Lottery tee shirts and mugs, or through joint promotions with other companies, must be shared with the NLDF.

• The above information is an extract from the National Lottery Commission's Lottery Guide which is available on their web site which can be found at www.natlotcomm.gov.uk

© *National Lottery Commission*

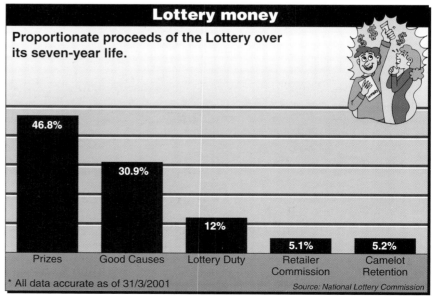

Lottery money

Proportionate proceeds of the Lottery over its seven-year life.

Prizes	Good Causes	Lottery Duty	Retailer Commission	Camelot Retention
46.8%	30.9%	12%	5.1%	5.2%

* All data accurate as of 31/3/2001

Source: National Lottery Commission

Gambling behaviour in Britain

Summary of findings from the British Gambling Prevalence Survey

Introduction

This report presents results from the National Centre's British Gambling Prevalence Survey. This is the first nationally representative survey of its kind in this country, and its overall aim is to provide baseline data on adult gambling behaviour in Britain. A random sample of 7,680 people (aged 16 and over) participated in the survey.

Over the past decade, the nature of gambling in Britain has been changing, due largely to the introduction of the National Lottery, but also to the increasing availability of other forms of gambling such as spread-betting and gambling on the Internet. While there is growing interest in the social impact of these new forms of gambling on the British population, up till now there has been little reliable information available about people's gambling behaviour. An important aim of the British Gambling Prevalence Survey was to provide statistically robust data on adults' participation in gambling, and to estimate the extent of 'problem gambling' within the country.

Participation in gambling activities

- Almost three-quarters (72%) of the population – that is about 33 million adults – took part in some form of gambling activity within the past year.
- Over half (53%) of the population – or about 24 million adults – gambled in the week prior to the interview.
- By far the most popular gambling activity is the National Lottery Draw. Two-thirds (65%) of the population bought a National Lottery ticket during the past year, while nearly half (47%) the population played in the week before the interview.
- The next most popular gambling activity is the purchase of scratchcards, with one in five people (22%) purchasing scratchcards in the past year. The proportion buying scratchcards in the week prior to interview was 8%.
- Among the other forms of gambling available, the next most popular activities are: playing fruit machines (14% did so in the past year), betting on horse races (13%), and making a private bet with a friend or colleague (11%). The proportions participating in these activities in the past week were: 6% for fruit machines, 3% for horse races and 4% for private bets.
- Fewer than one in ten people participated in the other types of gambling activities available: 9% of the population played the football pools in the past year; 8% played a lottery (other than the National Lottery); 7% played bingo; 3% played cards, dice or roulette in a casino; and 3% placed bets with a bookmaker (on events other than horse or dog races). The equivalent figures for the week before the interview were: football pools (6%); a lottery other than the National Lottery (4%); bingo (4%); casino gambling (less than 1%); and bookmaker betting (1%).
- The other new types of gambling were very much a minority interest: within the past week, no more than 1% of the population had done 'spread-betting' or had gambled via the Internet.
- Compared with many other countries which have carried out similar studies of gambling behaviour, it appears that the British are less likely to gamble. For example, the 72% of British adults who gambled in the past year is lower than the nine in ten adults in Sweden and New Zealand who gamble, and the eight in ten Australian adults. However, at 63%, it seems that adults in the United States are less likely to gamble than the British.
- Among those who have gambled in the past year, over two in three participated in only one (42%) or two (27%) different activities. In fact, one-third (35%) of those who gambled in the past year only bought tickets for the National Lottery Draw.
- While people's interest and participation in gambling lies on a continuum, a cluster analysis identified four broad groups of people: the 28% of the population

who were 'non-gamblers' in the past year; a third (33%) of the population whose participation in gambling is limited to the National Lottery Draw and/or scratchcards (referred to as 'minimal interest gamblers'); another third (32%) of the population who participate in one or two activities in addition to the National Lottery ('moderate interest gamblers'); and a small group (7%) of people who bet on a greater number and more diverse range of gambling activities ('multiple interest gamblers').

Who gambles?

- Men are more likely than women both to gamble (76% of men and 68% of women gambled in the past year) and to participate in a greater number of gambling activities (1.9 per year and 1.3 per year, respectively).
- The only gambling activity that women are more likely to participate in than men is bingo. Men are more likely than women to play the football pools and fruit machines, bet on horse and dog races, and to make private bets with friends.
- Gambling is most common among people in the three age groups: 25-34, 35-44 and 45-54 (around 3 in 4 people in this age range). Participation then declines to 66% at ages 65-74 (which is the same proportion as among 16-24-year-olds), and to 52% among people aged 75 or more. On average, people in the older age groups also gamble on fewer types of activities: for example, one-third (32%) of 25-34-year-olds participated in 3 or more activities in the past year compared with 10% of people aged 65 or more.
- By far the most likely to have gambled in the past year were people in paid work, while the least likely were those in full-time education.
- While gambling is a popular activity among people from all social classes, the type of gambling activity people participate in varies by social class. For example, people in Social Class I were the least likely to buy National Lottery Draw tickets (56% did in the past year compared with 69% of people in Social Class IIIM). While people in Social Class I were more likely to go to casinos (5%) than to play bingo (3%), the opposite was found among people in Social Class V who were far more likely to play bingo (20% did in the past year) than to go to casinos (only 1%).
- People living in households with low incomes (under £10,400 per year) were the least likely to have gambled in the past year, although two in three people in these households still did so. However, in general, levels of participation in gambling activities tended to increase along with household income (at least until around the level of £36,000, after which participation levels steadied, and even declined slightly).

Expenditure on gambling activities

Collecting accurate information on how much money people 'spend' on gambling is very difficult for a number of reasons. Firstly, 'spend' can be defined in a number of ways (e.g., amount staked, amount lost, etc.), and the interpretation is likely to vary for different people as well as for the diverse types of gambling activities. Secondly, it is known that people tend to overestimate their winnings and underestimate their losses at gambling. Thus, the survey results are able to provide only relatively crude estimates on gambling expenditure.

In order to collect expenditure information, a distinction was made within the questionnaire between two broad types of gambling activities. For four activities (National Lottery Draw, lotteries other than the National Lottery, the football pools and bingo tickets), information was collected on past week 'stake', that is the amount bet on an individual event (e.g. a horse race, a lottery ticket). For these four activities, results are presented for average stake as well as showing a distribution for the amounts bet in the past week. For all the other activities, information was collected

Primary mode of client gambling by age

Off and on course betting as the primary mode of gambling was found across most of the age ranges but particularly among those aged 36 and above. Problem gambling in casinos was also largely a primary mode for older clients. In the younger age categories, however, gambling machines continued to be the main problem area. There was one instance of a client who was consistently betting under the legal age of 18.

Source: GamCare 2000 Report

on 'net expenditure', that is the amount gambled minus any winnings. However, in order to keep the questionnaire as simple as possible, no information was collected on the amount won on these activities. Thus, for the majority of activities, it is not possible to calculate an average net expenditure, but only to show the distribution of losses for people who gambled on the activity in the past week. All the expenditure estimates are based only on people who had participated in the relevant activity in the week prior to interview.

- First, looking at the four activities where stake was collected, the average stake ranged from £2.80 per week for the National Lottery Draw to £7.20 per week for bingo. The percentage of people who spent £10 or more in the past week was also considerably higher among bingo players (21%) than for the other activities (e.g., only 4% of weekly bets on the football pools).
- Average stake was higher among men than women for the National Lottery Draw (£3.10 and £2.50 respectively) and the football pools (£3.30 and £2.00), but was higher among women on bingo tickets (£7.90 women and £5.10 men).
- For each of the activities, the majority of people who gambled in the last week reported that they won, broke even or lost less than £5: this was true for 94% of people who bought scratchcards; 78% on fruit machines; 77% on horse races; 57% on dog races; and 92% on bets with a book-maker (excluding horse or dog races).
- The percentage of people who lost £20 or more in the past week was: less than 1% buying scratch-cards, 3% on fruit machines, 4% on horse races, 7% on dog races, 4% on bets with a bookmaker (excluding horse or dog races).

Problem gambling

'Problem gambling' is gambling to a degree that compromises, disrupts or damages family, personal or recreational pursuits (Lesieur and Rosenthal, 1991). Unique among large-scale gambling studies, the British Gambling Prevalence Survey included both of the most commonly used screening instruments to measure current 'problem gambling' prevalence in Britain: the South Oaks Gambling Screen (SOGS) and the DSM-IV (Diagnostic and statistical manual of mental disorders, 4th edition). In accordance with most previous research, the thresholds used to classify 'problem gamblers' were 5 and above for the SOGS, and 3 and above for the DSM-IV. The two screens provide slightly different estimates of the prevalence of problem gambling in Britain.

A number of caveats should be taken on board when considering these estimates (for example, the potential inaccuracy of the screen-ing instruments, sampling bias and error, response bias, and the possibility of dishonest reporting). Thus, while by no means con-clusive, the findings from the British Gambling Prevalence Survey should be seen as a 'best estimate' of the prevalence of adult problem gambling in Britain.

- Among the population aged 16 and over, the prevalence of problem gambling in Britain is 0.8% according to the SOGS and 0.6% according to the DSM-IV.
- The likely number of problem gamblers in Britain is thus 370,000 according to the SOGS, and 275,000 according to the DSM-IV.
- Looking only at people who have gambled in the past year, the prevalence of problem gambling among this group is 1.2% accord-ing to the SOGS and 0.8% according to the DSM-IV.
- Compared with other countries which have used similar measures, the prevalence of problem gamb-ling in Britain appears to be relatively low (0.8%), at least in comparison with Australia (2.3%), the United States (1.1%), New Zealand (1.2%) and Spain (1.4%). On the other hand, at 0.6%, Sweden has a lower estimate of problem gambling than Britain.

Profile of problem gamblers

- The prevalence of 'problem gambling' varies depending on the type of activity people gamble on. The lowest levels of problem gambling were found among people who participated (in the past year) in the two most popular types of activities: the National Lottery Draw (SOGS 1.2%) and scratchcards (SOGS 1.7%).
- The highest prevalence of problem gamblers was found among people who, in the past year, had played table games in a casino (SOGS 8.7%) or who bet on sports or events (excluding horse or dog races) with a bookmaker (SOGS 8.1%).
- As might be expected, there was a higher prevalence of problem gamblers among the 'multiple interest' group, compared with 'moderate' or 'minimal' interest gamblers (SOGS 5.7%, 1.3% and 0.1% respectively).
- Multivariate analysis revealed that 'problem gambling' was statistically associated with the following socio-demographic factors: being male, reporting that a parent was or had been a problem gambler, and being in the lowest income category. An additional factor, being separated or divorced, was significantly associated with being a 'problem gambler' as measured by the SOGS (but not DSM-IV).

- The above information is the executive summary of a report by the National Centre for Social Research called the British Gambling Prevalence Survey, details of which can be found on their web site at www.natcen.ac.uk The survey, sponsored by GamCare, was conducted by Kerry Sproston, Bob Erens and Jim Orford.
© The National Centre for Social Research

Chips with everything

Internet users want entertainment and websites want to make money. Big online casinos are the perfect solution. As Aspinalls launches its own version today, Amy Vickers considers how the sector is finally becoming reputable

In a world full of uncertainties, there are just two sure things left on the internet these days – sex and gambling. Sex has been done to death with recent stories of out-of-work dot.commers turning to porn websites to bring home the bacon, and Yahoo's big porn dilemma. But gambling, in particular the entertainment side of gambling – casinos – is just starting to emerge as a mainstream internet pastime. It has been held back, however, by the struggle for respectability.

Casino behemoth Aspinalls, which launches Aspinalls.com today, has put all its chips on its family name making it stand head and shoulders above the thousands of cowboy casino websites out there.

Its emphasis is on trust, says Russell Foreman, chief executive of Aspinalls Online. 'It's all about making people feel comfortable. There's no way we'd do anything to jeopardise our reputation,' he explains. The fact that Aspinalls.com is also the first publicly traded online gambling organisation in the UK, and thus has City shareholders to answer to, means that it is not going to do anything that might turn the public against it.

Foreman expects rapid growth for the business and says it's the perfect time to launch a big online casino, because internet consumers want entertainment, and websites want to start making money. With the web evolving to become an entertainment medium, the challenging gaming factor of casinos is guaranteed to pull in punters – even if they haven't got the nerve to play for money.

The games on offer are carbon copies of those found in ordinary casinos, such as blackjack, poker, roulette and craps. Croupiers are replaced by clever software that generates the numbers randomly. The more accountable online casinos

By Amy Vickers

make a big effort to ensure that these systems are subject to stringent control systems. Aspinalls.com, for instance, is to be audited regularly by PriceWaterhouseCoopers.

> *With so many casinos on the web, it's difficult to determine which ones are honest and which are out to rip off consumers*

Many casinos ask players to download software onto their computers for faster and better play and set up accounts with credit cards, although most allow punters to play

for free first to get the hang of the games.

But with so many casinos on the web, it's difficult to determine which ones are honest and which are out to rip off consumers. Gaming bodies suggest punters stick with well-known names, such as Ladbrokes (ladbrokescasino.com) and Victor Chandler (thespinroom.com), rather than the lesser known ones that don't offer guarantees of audits.

Now that more and more transparent casinos are launching online, it is forecast that this market segment will represent a major area of growth, particularly when the inevitable happens and they are granted UK licences.

New research bears this out. Peter Tyson, an analyst at Datamonitor, expects online casinos to grow at a much faster pace than any other subset of the online gambling market. 'We're projecting

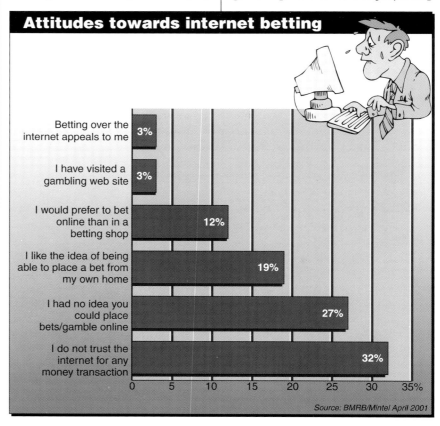

Attitudes towards internet betting

Statement	%
Betting over the internet appeals to me	3%
I have visited a gambling web site	3%
I would prefer to bet online than in a betting shop	12%
I like the idea of being able to place a bet from my own home	19%
I had no idea you could place bets/gamble online	27%
I do not trust the internet for any money transaction	32%

Source: BMRB/Mintel April 2001

a 40% growth rate for online casinos over the next five years, compared to just 20% for online sports betting,' says Tyson.

Datamonitor says the UK online casino market accounts for around 40%, or almost £300m, of the online gambling market. By 2004, this is expected to have grown to 50% of the market, or £760m.

So it is no wonder that suddenly a whole batch of online casinos is cropping up. No sooner had Aspinalls starting publicising Aspinalls.com than MSN sent out a press release about its very own casino, provided by Harrods. The combination of Bill Gates and Mohamed Al Fayed cosying up together may be too much for most people to stomach, but nonetheless it's another key deal that will do wonders for the widespread acceptance of online casinos.

MSN, the world's most popular portal, is hoping to ease some of its revenue problems by offering a link to the Harrods Casino. It will pick up 10% of all gambling revenues referred to Harrods by MSN links and marketing. Sources within the online casino industry also suggest that Freeserve has for some time been looking at putting together a similar deal with a reputable casino operator.

In little more than six months, Harrods has established itself as one of the best-known online casino businesses, and the strategic two-year marketing deal with MSN, which kicks in later this month, can only serve to bring in more punters.

The Harrods Casino, a joint venture between the department store and Gaming Internet, is already proving to be Gaming Internet's principal revenue generator, according to a spokesman. Figures should be out soon, but early end-of-year analyst projections suggest that the casino should have generated £7.5m by this September.

Gaming Internet is one of a handful of technology companies that supply ready-made online casino systems to famous brands. Other big suppliers include Microgaming, Cryptologic and Boss Media, which are starting to make headway in the UK now that more and more traditional brands want to get involved. Gaming Internet already runs an online casino for FHM.com and is developing a casino for the Paris Ritz Hotel called ParisRitzCasino.com.

Given the ease with which companies can launch an online casino, it's no wonder that there is a glut of casino websites. But as more and more reputable companies get involved and take the lion's share of punters, the number of fraudulent websites should, in theory, dwindle.

It's not difficult to work out how online casinos make money. Once people are hooked on the games, and they realise how easy it is to play, they become regular players

---

'People are very concerned by how easy it is for companies they have never heard of to set up an online casino, and then rip them off,' says Mark Brechin, author of a soon-to-be-released Mintel report on online gambling. 'That's why the brand is absolutely vital and why reputable brands have to operate transparent and audited casino websites.

'Aspinalls' launch should do well thanks to the respect its brand has established over the past 40 years. However, there are still loads of shady sites out there ready to relieve the unwitting punters of their folding money,' adds Brechin.

The reason 'brand' is so important is that there is no real protection for consumers. The legalities of online casinos are sketchy, with most companies locating their servers and businesses overseas to circumvent antiquated gambling laws. Laws are gradually changing, however. The casino operators want the UK gaming laws to be extended to protect consumers, and the government is thought likely to publish recommendations that should regulate online casinos and make them legal. Pundits are expecting the government, which loosened up the online gambling tax laws in the March 2001 budget, to clarify the antiquated online casino rules that are so prohibitive.

The most radical reform should be a single regulatory body set up to oversee the whole industry, effectively pooling the powers of the Gaming Board, the national lottery commission, the Jockey Club, the British Horseracing Board and the financial services authority.

The Gaming Board, the current regulatory body responsible for online casinos, is calling for a change in the regulations permitting online casinos in the UK. The reason companies go to the Caribbean, Central America and Gibraltar is that the governments of these territories are only too happy to grant licences in exchange for £100,000 for the licence and then tax on the turnover of the company.

Another key reform is expected to be the change in licensing laws, so that operators can be granted licences by a UK authority and don't have to purchase an offshore licence, or locate their servers abroad.

It's not difficult to work out how online casinos make money. Once people are hooked on the games, and they realise how easy it is to play, they become regular players. Loyalty systems are a big feature of online gambling and the theory is that regular gamblers can easily be persuaded to use their accounts to have a punt on sporting events.

The next step, casino games on interactive television and on mobile phones tied into betting, is the final piece of the jigsaw for big casino players such as Aspinalls, turning us all into armchair roulette wheel addicts.

• The above article first appeared in the *Guardian* Newspaper.

© Amy Vickers

On-line gambling

Information from the Department for Culture, Media and Sport

We have used the term on-line gambling to refer to gambling services that use a telephone connection. This includes services that are accessed via the internet, interactive television and mobile phones. Much of the current focus tends to be directed at gambling on the internet and increasingly via interactive television. The terms that others have used to describe the same activities include internet gambling, virtual gambling, interactive gambling and so on, as well as on-line gambling.

Generally on-line gambling is characterised in two ways: on-line betting and on-line gaming. Betting, pools and (some) lotteries which receive entries on-line but where the event, draw or competition occurs off-line are referred to as on-line betting. The gambling event actually takes place and the result is independently verifiable i. e. the on-line system does not generate the result, it is used simply as a conduit for communicating information. The internet is often an alternative to other means of entry such as the post or telephone. On-line gaming is used to refer to gambling services conducted purely on-line which rely upon some kind of random number generator. It may appear as virtual casinos, (some) lotteries and electronic gaming machines.

Regulation

As the Gaming Board has stated, gambling legislation – apart from that setting up the National Lottery – is all over a quarter of a century old and was enacted at a time when the power of the internet could not have been imagined. The legislation therefore impinges on on-line gambling in ways which were unintended and are erratic.[1]

The current legislation is thought to apply as follows:

- casino, bingo and machine gaming. It is illegal to set up on-line sites in Great Britain. Operators licensed by the Gaming Board to offer casino gaming, bingo and gaming machines must do so on licensed and registered premises. In particular, the persons taking part in the gaming must be on the premises at the time gaming takes place. The Gaming Board have advised that no licence could be obtained by an operator wishing to offer on-line gaming services and that to set up such a site would be illegal.
- betting. A bookmaker may accept bets on-line. Some bookmakers have chosen to operate offshore to avoid paying general betting duty, rather than because there is any legal difficulty in operating onshore. Since bookmakers are able to take bets via the telephone, it is accepted that they can take bets on-line.
- lotteries. Tickets for lotteries can be sold almost anywhere other than the street, however they cannot be sold by machine. The Gaming Board has approved two applications to run lotteries on the internet, having satisfied itself in those cases that the sale of tickets would be effected by sales staff and not machine.
- pool competitions. Football pools accept entries by post and can therefore also use e-mail.
- National Lottery. The National Lottery Act allows the sale of tickets from an attended machine.
- punters. Although operators are restricted by current legislation, no regulation prevents players accessing gaming or betting sites anywhere in the world. Nor is it illegal for overseas operators to offer on-line gambling to British residents (though there are restrictions on advertising).

Punters

The data available suggest that to date, only a tiny percentage of people have gambled on-line. The Prevalence Survey found that less than 0.5% of respondents had gambled over the internet.[2] Similar percentages have been reported overseas. Australian data suggest that in 1998-99 about 0.6 per cent of adults, nearly 90,000 Australians, gambled on the internet.[3] It has also been reported that of the 90 million web users in the United States, some 5% have gambled on-line.[4]

Identifying the type of person likely to gamble on-line is highly speculative. The betting industry told us that the profiles of telephone punters and betting shop punters are different so it would not be surprising if a typical on-line gambler also

differed from his off-line counterparts. The profile of an on-line gambler may be similar to that of a current e-commerce customer which is in turn based on analysis of internet users. The typical e-commerce consumer in the UK is said to be a 34-year-old male, in social class ABC1, who lives in the South East and has at least one degree.[5] Industry analysts have commented on the ability of interactive television to reach novice punters, such as women, younger people and ABC1s who would not normally enter a betting shop.[6]

There are varying estimates of the current number of people with on-line access via a PC, mobile phone or digital television, or likely to have access in the next few years. About 34% of households in the UK have internet access and around 30% of households have digital television, though only 10% of these use it for internet access and 15% for e-mail.[7] Current mobile phone penetration exceeds 70% though most phones are not internet enabled.[8,9]

Forecasts of the growth in on-line users are highly speculative but suggest that by 2005 mobile phone penetration could exceed 80% (and most of these phones will be able to access the internet) and penetration of digital TV could reach over 60%. In addition, individuals are already able to access the internet from their workplace and public locations, such as internet cafés and libraries and this is likely to become more commonplace. The availability of on-line services is likely to increase rapidly over the next five years such that anyone who wishes to access them should have no trouble in doing so.

Number of users

There are limited data available on the number of people registered with on-line gambling sites. Blue Square, which was launched in May 1999, reportedly has about 110,000 users registered on its onshore internet site.[10] Over the Grand National weekend, it is thought that it received over 70,000 (worldwide) bets on-line.[11] By March 2001, the interactive television site Open had signed up more than 20,000 betting cus-

tomers.[12] On-line betting sites apparently rank among the most visited entertainment sites.[13]

The industry

On-line gambling services accessed by consumers over the internet, via a mobile phone or digital TV network are a relatively new development. In the latter two cases bespoke gambling services may be offered instead of or in addition to services available on the internet. In time, other devices such as games machines, personal digital assistants (PDAs) etc. will provide connectivity to the internet and so potential access to gambling services.

Whilst the telephone is readily available, it is only suitable for transactions (e.g. placing bets or buying lottery tickets) in situations where the gambler already has a considerable amount of information about the gambling event. The interactive transmission of text and visual information offered by other networks/devices, in particular the internet, allows a much wider range of gambling services, including gaming as well as betting, to be provided.

Operators

It is difficult to say how many on-line operators exist because there is no requirement for registration. Theoretically all on-line sites are accessible by punters based in Britain. Many betting operators with bookmaking permits have offshore sites. Currently, they may use British-registered web addresses and divert the punter to an offshore site.

Although on-line casino gaming is not legal in the UK, British residents have access to the sites wherever they are. Some estimates suggest that there are around 1,500 on-line casinos in the Caribbean

alone.[14] Overall, there are already hundreds and possibly thousands of gambling websites around the world, all potentially accessible by British punters with internet access.

Estimated turnover

Present and future on-line gambling revenues are difficult to estimate because of the lack of verifiable public data.[15] Europe Economics estimated the value of the UK internet betting market to be in the region of £100m in 1999. This compares to a betting office turnover of £6,563m and telephone betting of £729m onshore and £250m offshore.[16] BSkyB announced that it made £33m from gambling in the second half of 2000, generated by the Surrey Group internet site and via Open, the TV-based e-commerce platform, which currently carries Blue Square.[17] Reports suggest that less than 5% of betting in the UK has gone on-line.[18] Other commentators have suggested that on-line betting now makes up 2-3% of the UK gambling market.[19] It is possible that very few people are betting on-line but it is the higher spending punters doing so.

The National Gambling Impact Study Commission (NGISC) Report on gambling in the United States quoted estimates that internet gambling revenues were $651 million (£434 million[20]) for 1998, more than double the estimated $300 million (£200 million) from the previous year.[21] The Netbets report stated that approximately 14 corporations were involved in on-line gambling in Australia in March 2000 and that much of their turnover was generated by overseas gamblers. One of the corporations reported a turnover of $100 million (£40 million[22]) in 1998-99.[23]

Commentators suggest that there will be a massive growth in revenues from internet gambling in the next few years but predictions of the likely size of the market vary enormously. A report produced by the National Office for the Information Economy in Australia estimated that the global market could be worth between $11 billion (£7.3 billion) and $110 billion (£73 billion) in annual turnover.[24] In their evidence to us, Christiansen Capital Advisors

LLC estimated that internet gambling expenditure would be in the region of $2.2 billion (£1.5 billion) in 2000 and $6.4 billion (£4.3 billion) in 2003. Whatever the exact figure, there is a significant internet gambling market both globally and in the UK.

References
1 Gaming Board for Great Britain (2000)
2 Sproston, Erens & Orford (2000)
3 Senate Select Committee on Information Technologies (2000)
4 Sutherland, J. (16 April 2001)
5 Retail E-Commerce Task Force (2000)
6 Broadband Media (9 April 2001)
7 Oftel (2001)
8 Mobile Communications (20 March 2001)
9 It is conceivable that mobile phone penetration could go over 100% in time particularly as it includes pre-pay phones no longer used
10 Broadband Media (9 April 2001)
11 Racing Post (13 April 2001)
12 Broadband Media (9 April 2001)
13 Ibid
14 Sutherland, J. (16 April 2001)
15 Kelly, J. M. (2000)
16 Europe Economics (2000) 28
17 Broadband Media (9 April 2001)
18 Ibid, 5
19 Merril Lynch (2001)
20 Using a conversion rate of (US)$1.50 to (GB)£1
21 National Gambling Impact Study Commission (1999)
22 Using a conversion rate of (AUS)$2.50 to (GB)£1
23 Senate Select Committee on Information Technologies (2000)
24 National Office for the Information Economy (2001)

• The above information is an extract from the *Gambling Review Report* produced by the Department for Culture, Media and Sport's Gambling Review Body. See their web site at www.gamblingreview.gov.uk

Take a gamble on digital betting

By Richard Kilgarriff

Two hundred years after Napoleon called us 'a nation of shopkeepers', digital media moguls are banking on us being a nation of gamblers, unable to go five minutes without having a flutter on the horses, the dogs, or the colour of Judy Finnigan's bra.

New technology has certainly made it easier for us to place a bet than ever before. At the bookies, on the racecourse (foot and mouth permitting), through the TV set-top box, mobile phone or PC. We can throw away money (which is the point of gambling) to our heart's content. But just because we can bet any time, any place, anywhere, does that mean we all will?

At first glance, the going looks good for the UK runners. BSkyB generated £33m in gambling revenues between July and December 2000. An aggressive and expensive roll-out of set-top boxes boosted this early lead and has got everyone in the new media industry jumping up and down with excitement. When the digital cable and terrestrial platforms join the race for the interactive gambling pound, through their own betting platform, the market dynamic will change.

According to media buying and research company Optimedia, the share of digital homes in 2005 will cross the line at 25.3% BSkyB, 23.6% cable and 7.6% DTT, with almost a third of the country remaining analogue until the latter half of the decade. That's a total of 14.1m digital customers paying an average of £5 each to take a 10% share of the UK's £7bn gambling market.

As a mass medium, TV can no doubt take the process of gambling into new areas of the social psyche

GamCare, an organisation which analyses the social impact of gambling in the UK, conducted a survey of 7,680 people in June 2000. The results described a nation of people who like to flutter in the company of other people, playing the National Lottery and bingo for instance, but who don't much care for solitary gambling. Of the 72% who had gambled in the last year 35% bet on the lottery. It's only when you get down to what the survey calls 'problem' gamblers, mostly men between the ages of 24 and 35, that the probability of taking a bigger slice of their wallet looks more likely to happen through the set-top box.

Enhanced TV does not necessarily produce enhanced viewers. Interactive evangelists will argue that viewers will bet on the outcome of an (exclusive) game or event as it happens on the screen, therefore generating 'live' revenues. All I can say to that is, imagine a group of English football fans betting against David Batty on the spot in 1998. Imagine that. Exactly.

As a mass medium, TV can no doubt take the process of gambling into new areas of the social psyche. If successful, TV betting may well make both men and women consider having a flutter more often, but channelling this new tendency may prove more difficult than its promotion. Betting online is quicker and open to offshore competition. Mobile betting between friends is more socially stimulating and accessible than the set-top box. So while no one will question the ability of the TV to change perception, in reality, it cannot control the way we live our lives.

Globally, however, the market for online betting looks huge. Investment bank Merrill Lynch says that the sector will be worth £125bn by 2015. Remember, though, 12 months ago the same bank also said Amazon would be worth $47.5bn. Today it is worth $3.5bn. So, while investment banks are not expected to be 100% right about their market valuations, we should at least expect them not to be 92.5% wrong.

In Las Vegas, the Mecca of the gambling world, the MGM Grand hotel has an entire floor of coin-operated Family Feud machines, immersing the Pearson TV brand into the heart of a real gambling community. Special cameras 'film' the gamblers and make them part of the game as they pay to play. How

this would translate online is immaterial. The point is that no one else can work that hotel floor with that brand and make that money from that community.

Using this as an analogy for the online gambling market in the UK, BSkyB, NTL, Telewest and OnDigital are the new hotels on the block. Their business is only as valuable as the number of new customers they attract through their doors in the next 10 years. The older hotels in this equation are the betting shops, the National Lottery and the bingo halls, who already have an established clientele.

In the battle for viewers and shareholder value, it seems that the digital players are unable to think outside the box when it comes to the promise of easy revenues from gambling. After building the multi-

channel market on exclusive access to sporting events, they are backing a horse with several riders in a field wide open to outsiders.

Today, in a fragmented media universe, the need for togetherness and communication has never been stronger – witness the popularity of messaging and mobile phones. The pleasure of gambling in groups is communal, tribal even. Its appeal goes deeper into the collective national character than a coin-operated slot machine or a button on the remote control. The British enjoy doing things together. They are also impossible to predict – as Napoleon once found to his cost.

• Richard Kilgarriff is managing director of iballs Media. The above article first appeared in the *Guardian* Newspaper. © *Richard Kilgarriff*

Play-as-you-view

Sky launches play-as-you-view interactive football gamble

The world's first interactive football television betting game was launched by Sky Sports yesterday, amid warnings that it could lead to an increase in gambling addiction.

The new game, Sky Play, allows fans watching at home to win money for correctly predicting the outcome and key moments of a match. Groups working with gambling addicts, however, believe the game does not contain any safeguards to prevent young people or compulsive gamblers from playing.

Sky Play comes in two parts. Using their remote controls, viewers can make predictions before a match in a number of areas such as scoreline, who will score, who will get booked first and how many corners and throw ins each team might take.

Once the game has started, viewers will also be able to predict the outcome of key moments, such as whether a free kick will result in a goal, a miss or a save, and whether a bad tackle will result in the referee booking a footballer, sending him off or taking no action.

By Vivek Chaudhary

Points scored are converted into cash prizes at the end of a match.

Sky Play is to make its debut at this Sunday's premiership match between Leeds United and Chelsea. The maximum prize is £3,000, with 50 runner-up prizes of £50.

Players hit a button on their Sky remote control and a call is made automatically via a satellite box. The call costs £1.50, flat rate.

Piers Croton, executive director of Sky Sports Active, said: 'While fans are watching the game they will have the chance to use

their skill and judgement to try to guess its outcome. It is something that football fans love to do anyhow.'

Groups working with gambling addicts warned that it was part of a wider trend of gambling games on television and the internet that was creating more addicts.

A spokesman for Gamblers Anonymous said: 'I cannot believe that a game is being set up that does not contain any safeguards over the participant's age. There is not even a password to ensure that only a certain adult can play. Children grasp new technology quickly and there's nothing to stop them playing.'

Sky Sports claims that there are enough safeguards, because viewers have to go through a series of steps before playing. Mr Croton said: 'We have relied on the normal disclaimers, which is ultimately that it is the bill payer's responsibility. There's nothing to stop anybody dialling a premium rate number and we have more safeguards than most of these.'

© *Guardian Newspapers Limited 2001*

Blackpool to be Las Vegas-on-sea

By Philip Johnston and Nigel Bunyan

Seaside towns could be transformed into Las Vegas-style casino resorts if the Government proceeds with a liberalisation of Britain's £40 billion gambling industry recommended yesterday.

A report from the Gaming Review Body proposed the first overhaul of gaming laws since they were tightened in 1968 because of the involvement of organised crime.

It wants to allow the building of giant casino hotels of the sort seen in Las Vegas or Atlantic City, initially in Blackpool.

There would be an increase in slot machine jackpots and an array of gaming restrictions would be swept away. Live music and alcohol would be allowed in casinos and bingo halls would be permitted to offer unlimited prizes.

However, there would be new curbs on gambling among the under-18s, with a ban on fruit machines in high street cafés and other unlicensed premises where young people gather.

The report also ruled out betting in pubs or alcohol on bookies' premises. It recommended the appointment of a Gaming Commission to enforce strict probity tests to weed out unscrupulous operators.

Tessa Jowell, whose Department of Culture has responsibility for gaming, said: 'Our present laws are badly in need of updating but reform must go hand in hand with tough, practical measures to protect young and vulnerable people.'

The proposals will be put out for consultation but are unlikely to become law for some time. Opponents of deregulation are concerned that it will swell the ranks of an estimated 400,000 gambling addicts but there are financial pressures for liberalised gaming laws.

The Treasury is facing big revenue losses as betting organisations base themselves offshore to take advantage of the growth in internet betting.

There are big rewards for the industry. A recent study by KPMG estimated the total amount gambled in the UK in 1998 was more than £42 billion, generating business worth £7.4 billion to the gambling operators.

Blackpool is already dreaming of becoming the Las Vegas of Europe, with plans for up to six casino hotels to replace most of the tacky frontage that is the Golden Mile. Each would have 1,000 bedrooms and huge centres accommodating 80 gaming tables and 2,500 jackpot machines with no limits on prize money.

'You could walk in off the street with a £1 coin in your pocket and win millions of pounds,' said Marc Etches, managing director of Leisure Parcs, the corporation that owns Blackpool Tower and already has a blueprint for the first casino hotel, Pharaoh's Palace.

'The prospects are incredibly exciting. We believe we can use gambling as the catalyst for Blackpool's revival. The resort could be the Las Vegas of Europe, although it could never be on the same scale.'

Leisure Parcs, whose proposals have the support of the local council,

claims the relaxation of the gambling laws could bring 25,000 jobs to Blackpool, as well as trebling visitor numbers to 30 million by 2020.

Alan Cavill, head of development at Blackpool borough council, shies away from the 'Las Vegas of Europe' label, preferring to see the proliferation of gambling as 'a tool of regeneration'.

He said: 'We are not talking about seedy, dark casinos but architecturally stunning, multipurpose entertainment centres that happen to include gambling.'

Blackpool still pulls more than 10 million visitors a year but its share of the tourism market has declined over the past 30 years and it is showing its age. Mr Etches, whose casino hotel would include a 3,000-seat theatre, sees parallels between Blackpool and America's other honeypot gambling centre, Atlantic City.

Each started out as an affluent seaside resort with a similar climate. Each went into a gradual decline but gambling has rejuvenated the American city.

Josie Hammond, secretary of the Blackpool Hotel and Guest House Association, joined officials on fact-finding visits to both Las Vegas and Atlantic City and is behind the scheme – with some reservations.

She said: 'We've got to get away from the image of being cheap and cheerful. Cheerful is fine, but let's do away with the cheap.

'This idea would help keep us ahead, but it would only be one of the eggs in the basket. It would be lovely to have boulevard fountains and pirate ships firing at each other, as in Las Vegas.

'But remember, it's the Irish Sea out there. In winter we have difficulty keeping the illuminations up.'

Mega-casinos on UK horizon

Mega-casinos on UK horizon if calls for liberal gambling laws get official backing. Blackpool bets on rule change with plan for gaming hotels

Las Vegas-style casinos are expected to come a step closer to Britain when a government review to be released this summer backs a fundamental rethink of gambling laws.

Sir Alan Budd, former chief economic adviser to the Treasury and now provost of Queen's College, Oxford, is heading the inquiry. He is expected to conclude the laws are out of date and that restrictions on live entertainment inside casinos and on advertising should be relaxed.

Britain's casinos are governed by restrictive legislation introduced in 1968 after several scandals involving Mayfair casinos. It regulates how casinos can advertise, restricts the hours of opening and obliges new members to go through a 24-hour 'cooling off' period before they can play.

The gambling review, according to a leak to this week's *Economist*, is expected to recommend that a single regulatory board be set up to control casinos, bingo clubs, horse racing and the new industry of spread betting.

Only the national lottery, which is already covered by the national lottery commission, would remain outside its aegis. Changes to the lottery are specifically outside the remit of the official review.

The changing face of gambling in Britain is exemplified by the launch today of a proposal by Blackpool Challenge Partnership to build six Las Vegas-style hotel casinos on Lancashire's faded golden mile.

The £1bn regeneration scheme will be backed by the tourism minister, Janet Anderson, but its promoters are gambling that the Home Office review recommends a fundamental relaxation of the law. It is expected to report in June, after the election.

Blackpool's bid is modelled on Atlantic City in New Jersey, and the first of its mega-gaming hotels is scheduled to be Pharaoh's Palace,

By Alan Travis, Home Affairs Editor

with pyramids, sphinxes and obelisks, to be built by 2006.

Until recently, casino advertising was banned, and even now it is restricted to discreet ads in the classified columns of magazines and newspapers. The kind of mass billboard advertising used to promote Atlantic City and Las Vegas across the US is still banned.

Also prohibited is staging live entertainment and providing alcoholic drinks at gaming tables. While American and European casinos boast row after row of one-armed bandits, only 10 slot machines are allowed in each British casino and only eight games are allowed, including blackjack, roulette, craps and poker.

Ministers are believed to acknowledge that the current regulation is overbureaucratic and uncompetitive. Despite Gordon Brown's background as the 'son of the manse', the chancellor's decision

to scrap betting tax in his Budget is also expected to lead to a more liberal gambling environment.

Any further relaxation of the laws is expected to be accompanied by an expansion in treatment facilities for problem gamblers, tough controls on under-age gambling and measures to keep the industry free from money laundering operations and infiltration by organised crime gangs.

When the review was launched in December 1999, the junior Home Office minster, Mike O'Brien, said that in the 30 years since the current gambling laws came into effect social attitudes had changed, and the law was fast being overtaken by technological developments.

Betting figures

- Global gambling totals £986bn a year, £7bn in UK
- 35m visited Las Vegas in 2000 (up from 21m in 1990); Atlantic City had 33m visitors
- Nine of 10 largest hotels in world are in Vegas: The Bellagio, a £1bn copy of Lake Como, has 36 floors, 3,025 rooms and 400 suites
- In 1998, Americans spent more on gambling than on recorded music, theme parks, video games, spectator sports, and movie tickets combined
- An estimated 5.3m Americans are gambling addicts, and 300,000 in UK
- 300,000 Britons a year visit Las Vegas, more than from any other country in Europe
- 1m work in gambling in US; average wage is $26,000
- There are 116 UK casinos; the 23 in London account for 70% of takings. Total 'drop' (money exchanged for chips) in 1999-2000 was £3.1bn
- 72% of UK adults gambled in some way in 1999

Esther Addley

So gambling is safe.
You want to bet?

Sir Alan Budd wants reform of Britain's gambling laws. The live-and-let-live brigade are right behind him, but it's the have-nots who will suffer. By Cristina Odone

Beads of perspiration glisten on the man's forehead and above his grimly set mouth. He draws sharp, short breaths – almost hyperventilating as he leans forward, holding on to the table with a white-knuckled grip. He's pale, and his eyes are glazed.

A heroin addict going cold turkey? A pop star getting his rocks off with a bit of auto-erotic asphyxiation?

No. This is the gambler featured in a warning video shown at Gamblers Anonymous meetings across America. Once they've gone through their 'Hi, I'm Joe and I'm a gambler' routine, the 12,000 members of one of the fastest growing self-help groups either side of the Atlantic have to squirm through this celluloid depiction of their addiction.

Shame Sir Alan Budd wasn't forced to watch this alarming short. If he had, he might have hesitated before giving the green light to round-the-clock casinos, curry betting shops and Las Vegas of the north – a new-look Blackpool of jackpot machines, alcohol fountains and girls in bunny suits.

Budd is calling for Britain's restrictive gaming laws to be ditched. He wants gambling – a £42 billion-a-year industry that supports 170,000 employees – to be rehabilitated as a leisure activity on a par with bowling, golf or knitting.

His message is likely to fall on fertile ground. 'Don't tell me how I'm gonna spend my money, mate,' is a much-cherished motto. Nearly as seductive, indeed, as the 'something for nothing' mentality that gambling promotes.

The promise of winning unimaginable riches with the purchase of a £1 National Lottery ticket – or the deal of a card, or the spin of a wheel – has always been alluring. It's not so much a vote of confidence in Lady Luck as the thrill of cheating the system that galvanises many into buying a scratch card or playing the fruit machines.

> *It's not so much a vote of confidence in Lady Luck as the thrill of cheating the system that galvanises many into buying a scratch card or playing the fruit machines*

The lazy graduate who would rather smoke weed on the dole than sweat over accounts in the office; the long-term unemployed, who feels excluded from a society that focuses on work; the pensioner who feels lonely and lost in her arthritic boredom; all see gambling as the way out of a shoddy or painful reality. Why work, or try to challenge your status as a non-person, when a winning ticket will deliver you from the trap?

This pass-the-buck attitude runs counter to the Protestant work ethic that still informs Britain and its laws. For centuries the free churches have viewed alcohol and gambling as twin evils – the Reverend Adele Blakebrough, a Baptist minister, remembers that her father had to sign a pledge to give up 'strong alcohol and gambling' at the tender age of eight.

But her church's suspicion of gambling was rooted in social as well as theological concern: gambling, like alcohol, claimed the heaviest number of casualties among the lower middle classes, who traditionally constituted the free churches' rank and file.

The loss at a card table that a wealthy man could easily afford risked plunging his poor neighbour into bankruptcy and into ruin. This holds true today as it did at the time of John Wesley: the libertarians' live-and-let-live attitude, which underpins their current call for the liberalisation of the gaming laws, is simply the reckless selfishness of the haves with regards to the have-nots – let me play even at the cost of others' suffering.

But a vote for gambling is also a vote for the collective abdication of responsibility. Gambling allows you to duck the consequence of your actions: you do not rely on your will or your moral compass to act as the agent of your fortune. Your fate is down to the roll of a dice rather than to you.

This sinister passivity – which frees you of any commitment to doing good, for what's the use, as you are not the architect of your own or anyone else's destiny – belittles you. A gamblers' society, like a gamblers' den, is a casino where the only rule is that there is a winner and lots of losers. Everyone is reduced crudely to a lowest common denominator of dosh – you either have it or you don't. And money becomes the only engine in this seedy universe: the gambler need invest nothing but a few coins to reap rewards; time, energy and ingenuity give way to the pence and the pound.

Television is complicit in the creation of this grubby greed. Through its agency, the National Lottery has slowly legitimised gambling, dragging it from smoky dens filled with sleazy dames and cigar-chomping dons, to the relatively squeaky-clean television world of Anthea Turner and Philip Schofield. But divorcing the gambler from the slime-ball was just the first step in the television campaign to lure us into gambling.

The biggest growth area in interactive television is armchair betting. Goracing, a consortium of BBC, Sky and Channel 4, is investing in a deal with the horse-racing federation to bring live horse-race betting into your very own living-room. There will be talk of regulations, certainly, to monitor this proposed penetration of your home for their gain. But the outcome of the endless reams of legalese will boil down in the end to this: every day, anyone with access to a telly and a bob or two, will be able to place a bet.

You can see it now: the eight-year-old crunching popcorn beside his nan, the two of them cheering on Rainbow Lout as he gallops past the finishing line and earns them a quid each. An innocent new family entertainment? Or a first step on the road to the local Gamblers Anonymous?

It would seem that our public institutions – the Government, the media – are all in on the act: they think they've found the perfect way to milk our greed while simultaneously promoting it. And so, when it comes to dropping the restrictions on gambling, they're game. Are you?

• Cristina Odone is deputy editor of the *New Statesman*

• This article appeared in *The Observer*, 22 July 2001.

Britain rolled over by lure of the lottery

By Nicole Martin

Britain is becoming a nation of compulsive gamblers who turn to betting shops, scratch cards, casinos and the internet in the hope of making a fortune.

Within a few years, gambling has changed from a specialised activity for professionals to a mainstream pastime with an annual turnover of more than £27 billion, according to a study from Manchester Metropolitan University.

Images of the opportunities created by winning the lottery are also at the forefront of television programmes such as *At Home with the Braithwaites*, which features a family transformed when one of them wins £38 million.

Dr Ken Parsons, the report's author, accused the lottery of galvanising the gambling spirit. Launched in 1994 with its 'It could be you' slogan, it preyed on people's greed and made betting socially acceptable. He said: 'Advertising to date has been very slick and has been designed to make people think they have a good chance of winning the jackpot rather than the one in 14 million chance; or it has been designed to play upon people's charitable instincts, giving an impression of altruism.

'Such is this exposure to gambling on the consumer that several psychiatrists argue that lottomania is occurring, whereby increasing numbers delude themselves into thinking they have won the jackpot.'

Dr Parsons said that 75 per cent of adults bought lottery tickets, with the figure rising to 90 per cent in 'rollover' weeks when unclaimed prize money is included in the draw the following week. Although most participants bought tickets for 'just a bit of fun' or 'a flutter', Dr Parsons said there was serious cause for concern. Since the launch in 1994, Gamblers Anonymous had seen its calls rise by 17 per cent, with a fifth relating to the lottery.

A recent study of reformed gamblers identified serious problems associated with their previous addiction. More than half went without food and clothes to find the money to gamble while more than 80 per cent became involved in illegal activities including stealing. Around 95 per cent lied to their families and friends to hide their addiction while a third admitted a 'breakdown of family' life.

A spokesman for Gamblers Anonymous said the sitution was getting worse with online gambling. 'A person can now lose all his money from the comfort of his living room,' he said. 'More worryingly, all a child has to do is grab his father's credit card and he can become addicted too.'

Graham Sharpe, of the bookmakers William Hill, said the future of betting was 'very bright'. He said: 'The Grand National proved the biggest we had ever seen. Bookmakers had a £100 million turnover in just one weekend.'

A spokesman for Camelot, which operates the lottery, denied that lottery tickets were responsible for the rise of gambling in Britain. He said: 'Playing the National Lottery is not seen as hardcore gambling. Most see it as a harmless flutter. Recent research has shown that the lowest level of problem gambling was found among people who participated in National Lottery games. Of all the calls to GamCare, a national organisation for gamblers, only 0.8 per cent related to the lottery.'

A sure bet?

Use your head! How to control your gambling. Information from GamCare

A sure bet?

We all take risks. Gambling is a kind of risk taking.

It's also fun and entertaining.

You can gamble on lots of things. Opportunities to bet are everywhere. You can even gamble on the internet. Fruit machines and scratchcards are quite cheap and quick to play, so playing them can easily become a habit. Each time you win you may find that you spend your winnings on more 'goes'. If you're not careful, though, you can get totally hooked.

Is gambling bad for me?

Gambling can be great fun. But if you let it get out of control, it can take over your life. It can get to the stage where you're not able to stop until you've run out of money, or think of anything else other than gambling. You 'borrow' money from friends and never pay them back, and get irritable and shaky when you can't gamble.

Have I got a problem?

Be honest with yourself. Ask yourself these questions – do they describe you?

- Have I ever lied about my gambling, or lied to get money for gambling?
- Do I spend more than I can afford on gambling?
- When I lose money, do I want to gamble some more to win back my losses?
- Do I gamble because I can't handle stress or worries in my life?
- Do I think about gambling when I should be concentrating on other things?
- Have I ever skipped school, college or work to gamble?

If you answer 'yes' to any of these questions, you should be concerned about your gambling.

So what do I do?

Speak to someone you trust, like: a friend, teacher, parent, youth worker.

You can also phone the confidential GamCare Helpline 0845 6000 133. At the other end of the phone will be someone who knows what you're going through, and isn't going to judge you. They can give you real help and advice.

Be smart – deal with it

A gambling problem isn't going to go away on its own! You need to do something about it. Telling someone about your problem is the first step, but there are other things you can do to help beat the addiction:

- Stop running away from the problem and blaming others. Decide to deal with it yourself.
- Think about what makes you want to gamble. Is it because you're bored, stressed out, or unhappy?
- Stop gambling while you're trying to break the habit.
- Write down each day how you're

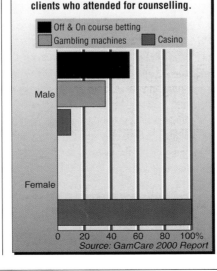

Gambling by gender

Off and on course betting was the primary mode for 54% of the male clients with gambling machines and casino gambling accounting for 36% and 10% respectively. Casino gambling was the exclusive primary mode for the small number of female clients who attended for counselling.

Off & On course betting
Gambling machines
Casino

Male

Female

0   20   40   60   80   100%
Source: GamCare 2000 Report

feeling and how you're coping.

- If you slip up, write down why you think it happened.
- Ask someone you trust to handle your money, at least until you've got your gambling under control. If you need money for other things, like food, clothes or fares, ask them for it and give them the change or receipts.
- Decide how you're going to start paying off debts.
- Cut up your debit or credit cash point cards.
- Treat yourself every now and then as a reward for not gambling. Spend some money on yourself!

You can beat the habit!

But it will not happen overnight. In fact, it may take some time before you really start feeling better. And it will be hard work. But keep going! Your confidence will grow every day you don't gamble.

You'll have days when you really want to gamble. Or you'll feel moody or depressed. But don't panic! Talk to someone about your feelings (remember the GamCare helpline!) and find something to do that'll distract you.

If you slip up and gamble, don't be too hard on yourself. No one's pretending that breaking the habit will be easy. Think about why the slip occurred and try to learn from what happened.

Take it one day at a time.

Find a hobby, sports activity or outside interest that'll get your mind off gambling and that you'll really enjoy. Try to do things with people who don't gamble.

- The above information is from a leaflet produced and published by GamCare, Suite 1 Catherine House, 25-27 Catherine Place, Westminster, London SW1E 6DU. Tel: 020 7233 8988 Fax: 020 7233 8977. E-mail: director@gamcare.org.uk Web site: www.gamcare.org.uk

Excessive participation

Information from the National Lottery Commission

In addition to ensuring that Camelot provides all players with a high standard of customer service, the National Lottery Commission has a specific duty to ensure that National Lottery games do not encourage people to play excessively. The Commission reviews all new games it is asked to license, and monitors the purchasing habits of players.

On-line games

On-line games (i.e. the Wednesday and Saturday Main and Extra draws and Thunderball™), which are characterised by relatively long gaps between buying a ticket, determining the results and then claiming any prize, are too slow to provide the immediate buzz that problem gamblers tend to seek. The fact that these are long odds games means that players are not encouraged, by frequent small wins, to chase their larger losses. Buying an on-line ticket is not a form of investment, and the National Lottery Commission guards against advertising that might encourage this view.

Instants™

Scratchcards were sold for many years before the arrival of the National Lottery. Unlike the on-line game, Instants™ do offer opportunities to play repeatedly, and their short odds prize structures offer many small prizes which players may choose to recycle by buying more tickets. Each application for a licence to promote a new Instants™ game is therefore evaluated particularly carefully. National Lottery retailers must not sell tickets to a person whom the retailer knows, or ought reasonably to suspect, plays excessively.

Monitoring

The National Lottery Commission monitors player participation and the results are published. It also monitors the work of others in the field of problem gambling. While there are arguments that the National Lottery has been the catalyst for changing

perceptions about gambling it does not appear to have encouraged excessive National Lottery play: reported household and personal expenditure is modest across all groups. However, the National Lottery Commission continues to be vigilant in this area.

If you are concerned about excessive gambling

GamCare, the National Association for Gambling Care Educational Resources and Training, was founded in 1997. Its core services are designed to promote responsible gambling, minimise problems, and develop facilities for those affected by gambling dependency. GamCare can be contacted at Suite 1, Catherine House, 25-27 Catherine Place, London SW1E 6DU; tel: 020 7233 8988. GamCare runs a confidential Helpline which can be contacted, for the cost of a local call, on 0845 6000 133. This is supported by confidential counselling services in London and elsewhere in the UK.

Under-16s

Young people may be more vulnerable than adults to the attractions of gambling. It is illegal for National Lottery tickets to be sold to or by under-16s.

Measures in place to prevent such sales include:

- restrictions on advertising.
- notices in retail outlets and on all National Lottery materials.
- the requirement for retailers to establish reasonable safeguards to avoid such sales (with strict sanctions, including possible termination of their contract for any offences).
- a programme of test purchases to test these safeguards.
- a hotline for people to report any information they may have on possible under-age sales (tel: lo-call 0870 160 0016).
- Proof of age card schemes.

The National Lottery Commission monitors the extent of under-age sales. A survey, published in February 1998, suggested that 7% of the young people sampled had been illegally sold National Lottery products in the week preceding the survey. Following a call for action from the then Director General, John Stoker, Camelot is taking steps to reduce this figure. Most welcome has been the introduction from April 1999 of a test purchasing programme by Camelot called 'Operation Child', which involves some 5,000 retailer tests per year.

• The above information is an extract from the National Lottery Commission's Lottery Guide which is available on their web site: www.natlotcomm.gov.uk

© National Lottery Commission

Gambling does destroy lives

I should know – my grandfather ruined his life, and his family's too

By Roy Hattersley

My views on gambling, I confess without embarrassment, were influenced by my upbringing. My maternal grandfather – who began life in the exalted trade of racing farrier – could not resist betting on the horses he shod.

He arrived late for his wedding because, having lost his fare home at the St Leger, he had to walk from Doncaster to his house on the Derbyshire coalfields.

Years of losing his shirt taught him nothing. Indeed, the obsession grew. At the end of his life, he gambled on anything – which fly would win the race to the top of the windowpane, or the hair colour of the next man into the pub.

My grandfather was hugely intelligent, brave and handsome. Gambling ruined his life and the life of his family.

But it is not only the stories of bills unpaid and bailiffs at the door – told to me by my mother – that make me regret the prospect of Britain's gambling laws being modified. I know that my grandfather was an extreme case.

But I also know how easily the temptation to 'have a flutter' or enjoy an exciting night at the casino can turn into an addiction.

The occasional Saturday evening at your local Napoleon or Josephine casino is, for most punters, a harmless laugh. Once the international gambling industry is given a free hand, it will reach out to the vulnerable and the unsuspecting.

Squander

Yesterday, Sir Alan Budd, notable free marketeer and sometime economic adviser to the Treasury, presented a report on the future of British casinos. It recommended an end to the rule which requires every punter to register membership 24 hours before he firsts watches the roulette wheel turn.

In short, the casual gambler – up for the Cup or wandering the streets after a row with his wife – can stroll in and squander his week's wages.

Casinos are also to be allowed to install unlimited numbers of slot machines, to woo their customers with sweet music and serve alcohol at the gaming tables.

And the Budd report has recommendations to make about other forms of gambling. Betting shops will be able to serve food (a clear encouragement to customers) and will be allowed to line their walls with one-armed bandits.

Inevitably, other sections of the gambling industry will demand the right to get their snouts into the same trough.

The bingo people have already demanded the right to increase the maximum permitted prize of £1 million, and repeated their complaint that, unlike the National Lottery – another form of gambling – they are not allowed to advertise on TV.

So what was once an old ladies' holiday pastime is about to become a form of mega-gambling.

It seems possible that Britain – having lost its steel and coal industries and most of its nationally owned motor manufacturing capacity – will become the gambling capital of Europe.

Restrictions on British gambling were originally imposed almost 40 years ago when it was feared, with good reason, that all sorts of hoodlums (including the Mafia) were waiting to move in on our casinos.

Nobody pretends that risk still exists. The problem now is not sawn-off shotguns but a gradual and corrosive destruction of the values on which our society is based.

Nobody can be sure the casinos will not become easy territory for drug pushers, but we can be certain that, once the international gamblers move in, they will be fertile ground for men who want to take money from people who cannot afford it.

It may well be that the Government – supported by the other political parties – welcomes the explosive expansion of the British betting industry.

Values

Only last year it announced a reduction in the betting tax in order to encourage the offshore bookmakers to come home.

That inducement worked. But, we have to ask, is it worth it? Will the sort of society which allows unrestricted gambling encourage the standards and values we want to inculcate into our children and grandchildren?

Calls to keep the lid on gambling will provoke Alan Budd – and people who parrot his libertarian philosophy without quite understanding it – to complain that supporters of un-relaxed restrictions want to create 'a nanny state'.

The same people are, even now, calling for the legalisation of cannabis. They quote John Stuart Mill, the great British philosopher of liberty: 'All errors which a man is likely to commit against advice and warning are far outweighed by the evil of allowing others to constrain him for what they deem to be his own good.'

Fine. Respect for the individual requires us to allow men and women to make their own mistakes. But, in a civilised society, there is no freedom to exploit others and no liberty to destroy families. Unrestricted gambling risks exactly that.

Liberty

Of course, Alan Budd, introducing his relaxation proposals, talked of 'increased choice for adults' – rather as Kenneth Clarke, selling tobacco in Vietnam, said smoking and the cancer it causes is a decision grown-ups must take for themselves.

But Budd admitted, by his assertion that he wanted to 'reduce opportunities for gambling by young people', that it is an addictive habit.

Even so, I would not prohibit the occasional flutter or close down the big city casinos, but that is quite different from creating the impression that Britain is the home of the gambling free-for-all.

The libertarian argument of 'let them do what they like and harm themselves if they must' can be tested against its most extreme manifestation. Naturally, that is to be found in the US where it is argued that, in a free society, men and women have the liberty to sell their body parts.

A judge – Mr Justice Candozo – ruled that human beings have absolute property rights over their organs, but 'a conspiracy of physicians has greatly reduced their value'. That,

> *Will the sort of society which allows unrestricted gambling encourage the standards and values we want to inculcate into our children and grandchildren?*

we can all agree, is libertarianism gone mad. But the principle it illustrates is irrefutable. Sometimes, restraints are necessary.

Indeed, one of the jobs of governments is to decide the limits of acceptable behaviour. Both the decision and the definition have to take account of the impression that new legislation creates.

If the Budd recommendations are endorsed, the message will go out that Britain is happy for Blackpool to become a poor imitation of Las Vegas and for every holiday resort to turn itself into a replica Atlantic City. I, at least, will regret the day that happens.

• The above article first appeared in *The Daily Mail*, September, 2001.

© Roy Hattersley

Confessions of an online gambler

Lisa Bachelor talks to Dan Boardley, an online gambler who is placing his bets on the internet

Dan Boardley, from Luton, is a regular online gambler – and as a spread betting trader, he can justify his gambling as being necessary research and part of his job.

A keen internet gambler, Dan hardly ever strays into the bookie's these days as the comfort of gambling from his desktop during the day rules out the need to face the once-popular betting office.

'The advantage of gambling on the internet is that it's tax free and most sites now offer a couple of free bets as an incentive,' Dan says.

Dan uses a number of internet sites to place bets but rates Eurobet, Sporting Odds and Odds Checker as his favourites.

'Some companies have racing as the main sport, while others may have a lot of prices on the cricket,' he says. 'It's a case of surfing the internet and finding companies which seem to offer what you're looking for.'

Dan says most sites are now relatively easy to use, and because he's regularly looking through the prices as part of his job, he gets a good feel for a safe bet. Tennis and horse racing are his favourites for a flutter and with Wimbledon coming up, he's spending more than ever.

'I usually bet between £10 and £20 a time, and I probably place about 10 bets a week. But with Wimbledon coming up, I am spending a bit more,' he confesses. 'The most extravagant bet I ever made was £70 on a 4-7 odds on tennis bet. Fortunately I won, as any bet over £50 is a lot for me.'

Although Dan is a keen online gambler, his hobby doesn't extend to interactive TV gambling – at least not yet. 'I might be interested in armchair gambling. At the moment the convenience of betting from my desktop at work is enough for me – but I certainly wouldn't rule out TV gambling in the future.'

© Guardian Newspapers Limited 2001

Signs, symptoms and stresses

Information from GamCare

A gambling dependency is difficult to spot. It has been called the 'hidden addiction' because:

- There are no physical symptoms as there are with drug abuse or alcoholism;
- Gamblers frequently do not believe they have 'a problem' or wish to hide it;
- Gamblers are exceedingly plausible and become adept at concocting believable stories to mask the truth;
- Money shortages and debts can be explained away with ease;
- With young people, gambling may be only one of several excessive behaviours.

There are, however, a number of signs and symptoms which, when taken together, indicate that gambling may be the problem. The more probable signs are listed in this article.

Many of these signs can also be applied to other excessive behaviours, so caution must be exercised before deciding that gambling is the problem.

Confirming that gambling is indeed the problem may prove equally difficult. Directly asking an individual if he or she has a problem is likely to lead to a flat denial. Talking with them about use of time, money and spending preferences, and their view of gambling in general is likely to be more effective. Friends or family, and perhaps tutor or employer can be further sources in confirming that gambling is the problem.

Signs and symptoms

1. Clear indications
- Request for help from gambler.
- Admission by gambler that he or she spends too much money on gambling.
- Gambler saying that they spend too much time gambling and cannot keep away.
- Gambling seen as legitimate means of making money.
- Persuading friends to gamble against their will.

- Gambling alone for long periods.
- Frequenting amusement arcades, betting shops, horse and dog tracks, or casinos several times a week.
- Spending excessive time playing on internet gambling sites.
- Spending more than they can afford on the Lottery.
- Committing crime to fund gambling or pay off gambling debts.
- Persistent reports that a person has been seen gambling and in the informer's view has a problem.
- Frequently in possession of fruit machine tokens, betting slips, scratchcards, etc.

2. Probable indications
- Money difficulties and debts that are cleared and then re-appear.
- Unrealistic suggestions to pay off debts.
- Criminal offences of fraud, embezzlement, and persistent theft of cash.

- No apparent interests, pastimes or leisure pursuits.
- High degree of knowledge about gambling.
- Blind optimism, looks at short-term prospects and is only concerned with the 'here and now'.
- Creates rows at home as an excuse to go out.
- Pockets/purse full of coins.
- Strenuous denial when challenged that gambling is a problem

3. Possible indications
- Parent(s) had gambling problem or gambled frequently.
- Need to show off skills or achieve group status.
- Poor school/work results compared to ability level.
- Truancy, college or work absenteeism.
- Dinner money misused – coming home persistently very hungry.
- Mood swings, irritability, restlessness.
- Very low, depressed, preoccupied, withdrawn.
- Lying to cover tracks or disguise money shortages.
- Lack of, or half-hearted interest

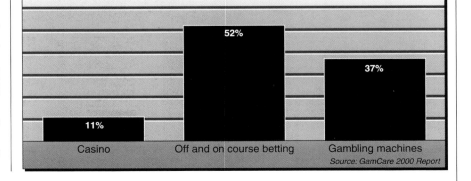

Primary mode of client gambling

The primary mode of gambling for the majority of clients was off and on course betting, accounting for 52% of presenting problems. However, there were significant increases in the numbers of clients whose primary mode was gambling machines (up from 27% to 37%) and also clients primarily gambling in casino venues (up from 2% to 11%). Unlike the previous year, spread betting (both sport and financial) did not figure as a primary presenting mode and only in a small way as a secondary mode.

Casino	Off and on course betting	Gambling machines
11%	52%	37%

Source: GamCare 2000 Report

Overcoming compulsive gambling

Professor Alex Blaszczynski has pioneered cognitive behavioural techniques to help people recover from gambling addiction . . . and countries all over the world now teach them. Here, he gives the foundations of an indispensable guide

It has long been acknowledged that excessive gambling incurs social and economic costs: poverty, starvation, family disintegration and criminal behaviour And we know that most people who gamble to excess develop psychological symptoms of depression and anxiety, that many turn to alcohol or drugs as a means of temporarily escaping their problems.

But do not despair. The cycle can be broken and recovery achieved.

What are the characteristics of problem gambling?

People who compulsively gamble to excess commonly report the following feelings.

Before gambling:

- increasing preoccupation with gambling, to the point where nothing else is important; this is often experienced as a sense of craving
- fear of losing an opportunity to win
- irrational confidence and fantasies about winning
- excitement in anticipation of the 'winning' ticket and fantasising about what to do with winnings
- irritation, anger and mounting tension if prevented from gambling

During gambling:

- all attention on gambling; all else fades
- excitement and physical arousal, shown by faster heart beat
- irrational talk inside their head: the next bet is the winner, it must be my turn to win next . . .
- superstitious behaviour to increase chance of a win

After a successful session:

- relief and anticipation of the next occasion

THE WINNER WOULD LIKE TO THANK ALL THE MILLIONS OF PUNTERS WHO MADE THIS FABULOUS WIN POSSIBLE . . .

- confidence and conviction that it was due to skill
- elated mood
- inflated ego, having 'beaten' others at their game
- self-satisfaction at having money and being able to impress a partner or spouse

After losing:

- guilt and remorse
- fear of spouse and others finding out
- worry over where to get money for living expenses
- thoughts of what lies to tell to cover one's actions
- determination never to gamble again – but at the same time, thoughts of where to find money to chase losses, and
- desire to forget problems through alcohol.

What signs can families and partners look out for?

Gamblers include all types of personality and all kinds of personality traits are found in gamblers. But there are general signs which partners and family members can look out for as signals that a problem might exist. These include:

- lengthy or unexplained times away from work and home
- complaints of poor productivity at work
- betting tickets suggesting large bets
- preferring to play slot machines alone instead of remaining in social company while out
- always being short of cash despite regular income
- having many credit cards with little available credit
- having multiple loans
- mood shifts coinciding with major race days
- preoccupation with studying the form guide, listening to races or watching race broadcasts
- friends who comment on the money they have lent
- calls from creditors or legal action for debts
- sudden job changes

- repeated bounced cheques
- money or items disappearing from the home, and
- discovering less money in the bank account than there should be.

For gamblers themselves, a good self-assessment is obtained by answering honestly 20 questions listed by Gamblers Anonymous. These include:

- Has gambling ever made your home life unhappy?
- Have you felt remorse after gambling?
- Did you ever gamble to get money with which to pay debts or solve financial difficulties?
- Did gambling decrease your ambition or efficiency?
- After a win, did you have a strong urge to win more?
- After losing, did you have an urge to win back losses?
- Did you gamble until your money was gone?
- Did you ever borrow to finance your gambling?
- Were you reluctant to use 'gambling money' for normal expenditures, including for your family?
- Have you ever gambled to escape worry or trouble?

Some of the best predictors of pathological gambling are the compulsion to chase losses, repeated failed efforts to stop gambling, and gambling in response to negative emotions such as stress and depression.

The goals of treatment: abstinence or control?

The motivation to cease gambling is externally driven. A few gamblers are aware that they must take action to prevent significant problems in their lives. But three-quarters of gamblers are pressured to modify their behaviour by their spouses, relatives or employers.

There are two main yet opposing principles of treatment: 'abstinence' and 'controlled' gambling. Gamblers Anonymous advocates abstinence. This can be taken to mean absolutely no participation in any form of gambling, including infrequent purchase of raffle/lottery/scratch tickets, and draws or office sweepstakes.

Abstinence is considered essential because of the belief that any gambling will result in a relapse and resumption of gambling patterns. GA believes that compulsive gambling is a chronic and progressive disorder which can never be cured but only arrested.

But a detailed reading of psychological and psychiatric literature reveals that many outcome studies refer to marked reduction in the frequency and intensity of gambling after treatment. Positive gains are made despite continued gambling at much reduced levels. This has led many researchers to evaluate the effectiveness of controlled gambling.

'Control' means that the gambler can place defined bets according to pre-arranged limits. In all the cases reported, the gambler's spouse was involved in financial management and supervision.

In a follow-up study over periods of two to nine years, it was found that a third of gamblers achieved controlled gambling over, on average, five years after behavioural therapy. This group showed a reduction in psychopathology, gambling expenditure and debt and improvement in quality of life, marital relationships and self-esteem.

Some abstinent gamblers had one or two lapses which did not lead to relapse or continued gambling.

A word of caution is in order here. While there is some suggestion that controlled gambling might be possible, we do not know how to differentiate between these gamblers who can achieve control and those who cannot. Nor do we know the factors which predict who will or will not resume compulsive gambling after a lapse. So it is imperative that

gamblers accept the necessity of abstinence as the preferred goal in the first instance.

How can relapses after treatment be prevented?

Relapse-prevention strategy has grown out of the study of addiction. Its main purpose is to teach people to see the chain of seemingly innocent links which gradually leads them to a high-risk situation with the likelihood of a relapse or 'bust'.

Once you have identified the conditions under which you are most likely to experience the urge to gamble, as well as the steps to take to change your course of action, and have learned how to seek support from others close to you, you are well on the way to continued long-term recovery. This means learning straightforward strategies which will:

- help you reduce your urge to gamble when it arises through relaxation techniques
- correct faulty logic and thinking which cause you to believe that you have special skills or control over the outcomes of chance events
- identify triggers which will provoke your urge to gamble, such as negative emotional states
- offer stress management and provoke your urge to gamble, such as negative emotional states
- offer stress management and problem-solving strategies which will give you alternative ways of dealing with stress, anxiety and depression, and
- teach you to avoid gambling-related cues.

If you want to know more . . .

Highly recommended by *Addiction Today*'s editor is *Overcoming Compulsive Gambling. A self-help guide using cognitive behavioural techniques* by Professor Alex Blaszczynski which contains not only the information in this article but many, vital strategies which all gamblers can use to recover from their addiction. It is available from Robinson (tel: 020 7938 3830) at £7.99. ISBN 1-85487-484-5.

© Addiction Today

Gambling FAQs

Information from Gamblers Anonymous

What is Gamblers Anonymous?
Gamblers Anonymous is a fellowship of men and women who have joined together to do something about their own gambling problem and to help other compulsive gamblers do the same.

What is compulsive gambling?
There are many and varying interpretations of compulsive gambling. The explanation that seems most acceptable to GA members is that compulsive gambling is an illness, progressive in its nature, which can never be cured, but can be arrested.

Before coming to GA, many compulsive gamblers thought of themselves as morally weak or just 'no good'. The GA concept is that the compulsive gambler is a very sick person who can recover by following a very simple programme, to the best of his or her own ability, that has proved successful for hundreds of other men and women with a similar problem.

What is the first thing a compulsive gambler ought to do in order to stop gambling?
To accept the fact that compulsive gambling is a progressive illness and to have the desire to get well. Our experience has shown that the GA programme will always work for anyone who wants to stop gambling. It will seldom work for the man or woman who cannot, or will not, squarely face the facts about this illness.

Only you can make that decision. Most people turn to GA when they become willing to admit that gambling has them licked. Also, in GA a compulsive gambler is described as a person whose gambling has caused growing and continuing problems in many departments of life.

Many GA members went through terrifying experiences before they were ready to accept help. Others were faced with a slow, subtle deterioration which finally brought them to the point of admitting defeat.

Can a compulsive gambler ever gamble normally again?
No. The first small bet to a problem gambler is like the first small drink to an alcoholic. Sooner or later comes the fall back into the old destructive pattern.

Once a person has crossed the invisible line into irresponsible gambling, then it seems to be impossible to regain control. After abstaining a few months, some of our members have tried some small bet experiments, always with disastrous results. The old obsession inevitably returned.

The GA concept is that the compulsive gambler is a very sick person who can recover by following a very simple programme, to the best of his or her own ability

---

Our GA experience seems to point to these alternatives; to gamble, risking progressive deterioration, or not to gamble, and develop a spiritual way of life.

Does this mean I can't even do the lottery or play a game for table stakes?
It means exactly that. A stand has to be made somewhere and GA members have found the first bet is the one to avoid, even though it may be as little as tossing for a cup of coffee.

Why can't a compulsive gambler simply use his willpower to stop gambling?
We believe that most people, if they are honest, will recognise their lack of power to solve certain problems. When it comes to gambling, we have known many problem gamblers who could abstain for long periods, but caught off guard – and in the right circumstances – they started gambling without thought of the consequences. The defences they relied upon through willpower alone gave way before some trivial reason for placing a bet.

We have found that willpower and self-knowledge will not help in those mental blank spots but adherence to spiritual principles seems to solve our problems. Most of us feel that a belief in a power greater than ourselves is necessary in order for us

to sustain a desire to refrain from gambling.

Do GA members go into gambling places to help former members who are still gambling?

Often families and friends of these people have asked us to intercede but we have never been able to be of any real help. Actually, sometimes we felt we held back a member's eventual recovery by giving this unsolicited attention. It all goes back to the basic principle that a gambler ought to want help before being approached by us.

I only go on gambling binges periodically. Do I need GA?

Only you can determine whether or not, or how much, you need GA However, most periodic gamblers who have joined GA tell us that, though their gambling binges were periodic, the intervals between were not periods of constructive thinking. Symptomatic of these periods were nervousness, irritability, frustration, indecision and a continued break-down in personal relationships. These same people have often found the GA programme a guide to spiritual progress towards the elimination of character defects.

If I stop gambling, won't it make it difficult for me to keep some desirable business and social contacts?

We think not. Most of the world's work of any consequence is done without the benefit of monetary wagering. Many of our leaders in business, industry and professional life have attained great success without knowing one card from another or which way the horses run round the course. In the area of social relationships, the newcomer will soon find a keen appreciation of the many pleasant and stimulating activities available – far removed from anything that is remotely associated with gambling.

If I join GA, won't everyone know I am a compulsive gambler?

Most people made quite a name for themselves as full-fledged gamblers by the time they turned to GA. Their gambling was not usually a well-kept secret. It would, then, be unusual if the good news of their abstinence from gambling did not cause comment. However, no disclosure of any affiliation with GA can rightfully be made by anyone but the member personally. Even then, it should be done in a way that will not harm the GA fellowship.

How does a person stop gambling through the GA programme?

This is done by bringing about a progressive personality change from within. This can be accomplished by having faith in and trying to understand the basic concepts of the GA Recovery Programme.

There are no short cuts to gaining this faith and understanding. To recover from one of the most baffling, insidious, compulsive addictions will require diligent effort. Honesty, open-mindedness and willingness are the key words in our recovery.

Can a person recover by himself by reading literature or medical books on the problem of compulsive gambling?

Sometimes, but not usually. The GA programme works best for the individual when it is recognised and accepted as a programme involving other people. Working with other compulsive gamblers in a GA group, the individual seems to find the necessary understanding and support. There is an ability to talk of past experiences and present problems in a comfortable area. Instead of feeling alone and misunderstood, there is a feeling of being needed and accepted.

Are there more compulsive gamblers in certain occupations than in others?

Among GA members, there seems to be a predominance of those who work on their own or have little personal supervision. Obviously this allows more freedom to gamble. The occupations of the other members, including those at school or at home, are extremely varied. It seems safe to say that compulsive gambling has nothing to do with the occupation or age of the individual.

It apparently arises from an inner imbalance, not external factors.

Does GA look upon compulsive gambling as a moral vice?

No.

Is knowing why we gambled important?

Not as a rule. Of the many GA members who have had extended psychiatric treatment, none have found a knowledge of why they gambled to be of value insofar as stopping gambling.

What are some of the factors that might cause a person to become a compulsive gambler?

GA members, in considering this perplexing question, feel these are some of the possible reasons:

Inability and unwillingness to accept reality. Hence, the escape into the dream world of gambling.

Emotional insecurity. Here a compulsive gambler finds emotional comfort only when 'in action'. It is not uncommon to hear a GA member say, 'The only place I really felt like I belonged was when I was in a gambling environment. There I felt secure and comfortable. No great demands were made upon me. I knew I was destroying myself yet, at the same time, I had a certain sense of security.'

Immaturity. A desire to have all the good things in life without any great effort seems the common character pattern of the problem gambler. Many GA members accept the fact that they were unwilling to grow up. Subconsciously they felt they could avoid mature respons-ibility through wagering on the spin of a wheel or the turn of a card and so the struggle to escape responsibility finally became a subconscious obsession.

Also, a compulsive gambler seems to have a strong inner urge to be a 'big shot' and needs to have a feeling of being all-powerful. There is a willingness to do anything (often of an antisocial nature) to maintain a personal image for others to see.

Then, too, there is the theory that compulsive gamblers sub-consciously want to lose to punish themselves. There is evidence among GA members to support this theory.

What is the dream world of the compulsive gambler?

This is a rather common characteristic of us compulsive gamblers when still gambling. We spend a lot of time creating images of the great and wonderful things we are going to do when we make the big win. We often see ourselves as charming and charitable fellows.

We may dream of providing our family and friends with new cars, expensive holidays and other luxuries. We picture ourselves leading pleasant and gracious lives made possible by the huge sums of money we will accrue from our 'system'. Servants, penthouses, charming friends, nice clothes, yachts and world tours are a few of the wonderful things that are just around the corner when we finally make a big killing.

Pathetically, however, there never seems to be a big enough win to make even the smallest dream come true. When we succeed, we gamble to dream still greater dreams. When we fail, we gamble in reckless desperation and the depths of our misery are fathomless as our dream-world comes crashing down.

Sadly, we struggle back, dream more dreams and, of course, suffer more misery. No one can convince us that our great schemes will not some day come true. We believe they will for, without this dreamworld, life for us would not be tolerable.

Isn't compulsive gambling basically a financial problem?

No, compulsive gambling seems to be an emotional problem. When in the grip of this illness, we create mountains of apparently insoluble problems. Of course, there are financial problems but we also have to face family problems, employment problems, or problems involving ourselves with the law. We lose our friends and relatives have us on their personal blacklist.

Of the many serious problems we create, the financial problems seem the easiest to solve.

Upon entering GA and stopping gambling, we find income often increases and, as there is no longer the financial drain caused by gambling, there is soon relief from the financial pressures.

The most difficult task to be faced is that of bringing about a personality change from within ourselves. Most of us in GA look upon this as our greatest challenge and believe this to be a lifetime job.

Does GA want to abolish gambling?

No. The question of abolishing gambling is a controversial issue about which GA has no opinion.

Who can join GA?

Anyone who has a desire to stop gambling. There are no other rules or regulations concerning GA membership.

How much does it cost to join GA?

There are no assessments in connection with GA membership. The newcomer signs nothing and pledges nothing. However, we do have expenses relative to our group meetings and our GA service facilities. Since GA has traditionally been fully self-supporting and declines outside contributions, these expenses are met through voluntary financial support by the members. Experience has shown that acceptance of these financial responsibilities is a vital part of our individual and group growth process.

Who runs GA?

GA is a unique spiritual movement having no central government and little formal organisation. There are no officers or executives who wield authority over the fellowship or the individual. Even though GA is an informal organisation, certain jobs have to be done.

In the local group, someone has to be responsible for the meeting place, look after the group finances, arrange for refreshments and keep in touch with other groups. This means that a group needs responsible people to perform these duties.

In accepting these responsibilities, a member may acquire a title, but titles in GA are used only to designate areas of service. Those who accept these responsibilities are directly accountable to those they serve.

Is GA a religious society?

No, GA is composed of people from many religious faiths, along with agnostics and atheists. Since membership in GA requires no particular religious beliefs as a condition of membership, it cannot be described as a religious society. The GA recovery programme is based on acceptance of certain spiritual values but the individual member is free to interpret these principles as he chooses.

As it is used in GA, what is the meaning of the word 'spiritual'?

Simply stated, the word can be said to describe that characteristic of the human mind which is marked by the highest and finest qualities, such as generosity, honesty, tolerance and humility. Inasmuch as the GA fellowship advocates acceptance of these principles as a way of life, it can thus be said that GA is a spiritual fellowship.

• The above information is an extract from Gamblers Anonymous' web site which can be found at www.gamblersanonymous.org.uk

Under-16s and the National Lottery

Information from the National Lottery Commission

Executive summary

This independent study was commissioned and administered by the National Lottery Commission. It was designed by Dr Sue Fisher, Director of the Centre for Research into the Social Impact of Gambling in consultation with the Social Research Division of the British Market Research Bureau (BMRB), and the National Lottery Commission. The report was prepared by Jacinta Ashworth and Nicola Doyle of the Social Research Division, BMRB.

Aims

The main aims of the research were to determine the level of underage sales of National Lottery products and the prevalence of 'problem gambling' by under-16s on National Lottery scratchcards, and to compare these findings with the Fisher (1997) survey. The research also attempted to explore whether under-16s understood the reasons for the age restrictions on the National Lottery.

Methods

The fieldwork was conducted from 7th June to 23rd July 1999. The sample of 9,529 12-15-year-olds was drawn from a representative sample of 111 schools in England and Wales. As in 1997, the mode of data collection was supervised, anony-mous, self-completion questionnaires. According to research this method may under-report risky behaviours in young people (Turner et al, 1998), but it is currently the most efficient method for obtaining data from large numbers of school pupils. Very large numbers are required for this type of research to obtain reliable statistics about subgroups of interest, such as young people involved in illegal sales and 'problem gamblers'.

Defining problem gambling

A small minority of people gamble in a way that compromises, disrupts or damages family, personal, or recreational pursuits. These people are called 'problem gamblers' (Lesieur & Rosenthal, 1991). It can be seen from this definition that the term 'problem gambling' describes a range of behaviour. This range of behaviour may be viewed as a continuum with the less severe cases at one end and the most severe cases at the other.

Screening for problem gambling

As the above definition suggests, problem gambling is a complex phenomenon, and not simply a matter of excessive expenditure on gambling. A problem gambling 'screen' is an index of behaviours and psychological states, known to be correlated with problem gambling, which is used to identify problem gamblers in a given population. The problem gambling screen used in this study is a version of the DSM-IV criteria published by the American Psychiatric Association (APA, 1994). The criteria were first adapted for use in juvenile populations by Fisher (1992) and since then have been used in youth studies in Britain (Fisher, 1993; 1995; 1997; 1999 & Wood & Griffiths, 1998), Spain (Becona & Gestal, 1996; Becona, 1997) and Canada (Gupta & Derevensky, 1998). Research shows that the youth-adapted DSM-IV screen is the most conservative measure in popular current usage (Derevensky & Gupta, 1997). It has nine items, positive responses to at least four of them being required for a classification of problem gambling.

Key findings

Illegal (underage) sales
Camelot's 'Project 16', launched following the 1997 OFLOT survey, was intended to reduce underage sales

through advice to retailers, test purchases and publicity about age limits. This study found that 'Project 16' may have had some effect. Although there was a significant increase in the proportion of under-16s spending their money on the National Lottery in the past week (see below), the proportion of illegal underage sales was virtually the same as for 1997.

- 7.0% of the under-16s surveyed reported an illegal sale in the week prior to the survey, not significantly different from 6.5% in 1997.

As in 1997, illegal sales were associated more with scratchcards themselves than other National Lottery products.

- 45% of the young people who had spent their own money on National Lottery scratchcards in the past week had been sold them illegally compared with 35% who had spent their money on the Draw and 36% who had spent their money on Thunderball.

Past week expenditure on the National Lottery (including legal and illegal sales)

This study found that since 1997 there has been a significant increase in the proportion of under-16s spending their own money on the National Lottery in the week prior to the survey. The figures for past week expenditure shown below include both illegal sales (where the actual purchase has made been made by a young person under 16 years) and legal sales (where an adult has handed over the money for them).

- 17.7% of 12-15-year-olds had spent their own money on at least one of three National Lottery games – Draw, Instants (scratchcards) or Thunderball – in the past week, compared with 13.5% in 1997.
- This increase was almost entirely due to an increase in the proportion of respondents who had spent their own money on National Lottery scratchcards (11.6% in 1999 compared with 7.7% in 1997).

Demographically, the following groups were more likely to have spent their money on the National Lottery:

boys, those who were nearer to being 16, and those with a higher disposable income. These factors were also inter-related: boys and Year 10 pupils (14-15s) tended to have more money to spend than girls and Year 8 pupils (12-13s).

The growth in past week expenditure since 1997 resulted mainly from growth in parental purchases on behalf of their children (legal sales) rather than growth in purchases by under-16s (illegal sales). Nevertheless, some 40% of the under-16s who had spent their own money on the National Lottery in the week prior to the survey made the purchases themselves (or a friend under the age of 16 made the purchase for them).

Problem gambling on National Lottery scratchcards

The study found a small, statistically insignificant, fall in the proportion of young people meeting the DSM-IV criteria for problem gambling on National Lottery scratchcards.

- 1.7% were classified as problem gamblers of Instants (2.3% in 1997).
- 69% of the problem gamblers of Instants were also problem players of fruit machines (the only other game to be screened for problem gambling) and many were past week players of other commercial games.

Past week commercial gambling by problem gamblers of Instants

The problem gamblers of Instants (n=166) were more likely than the non-problem gamblers of Instants (n=2760) to have spent their money in the past week on all of the following commercial games:

- National Lottery games (78% compared with 35%)
- fruit machines (72% compared with 37%)

- betting games through a betting shop (34% compared with 9%)
- bingo at a bingo club (28% compared with 5%)
- other commercial scratchcards (60% compared with 16%).

These findings are highly significant and suggest that, while they may favour one particular form, for some young people gambling per se is the problem.

'National Lottery Live' television programmes

The 'National Lottery Live' television programmes were watched by both players and non-players:

- 24% of all the young people surveyed watched the midweek show 'last time it was on'.
- 38% of all the young people surveyed watched the weekend show 'last time it was on'.

As in 1997, this study found that viewing these programmes was associated with a greater propensity to spend money on the games:

- 30% of those watching the last midweek show and 27% of those watching the last weekend show spent their money on a National Lottery game in the past week compared with 18% in the sample as a whole.

However, without qualitative research it is impossible to ascertain whether viewing increases the likelihood of spending money on the National Lottery or whether spending money on the National Lottery increases the likelihood of viewing. The most plausible explanation is that both are true.

Under-16s' understanding of National Lottery age restrictions

The young people were asked whether or not they agreed with a range of attitude statements on the potential negative effects of playing National Lottery games on young people. These statements were presented in the context of why there is an age restriction of 16 years in place.

- 72% agreed that 'it is easier to spend more money than you plan to on National Lottery scratchcards' (68% on the Draw).
- 80% agreed that 'some people become hooked on National

Lottery scratchcards' (77% on the Draw)

- 63% agreed that 'playing National Lottery scratchcards can lead to serious money problems' (64% on the Draw).

Even the problem gamblers of National Lottery scratchcards tended to agree with these statements:

- 60% of the problem gamblers of National Lottery scratchcards agreed that 'it is easier to spend more money than you plan to on National Lottery scratchcards', 61% agreed that 'some people become hooked on National Lottery scratchcards', and 48% agreed that 'playing National Lottery scratchcards can lead to serious money problems'.

Implications of the study

Controlling one's response to gambling requires certain life skills which are likely to be underdeveloped in children and young people. Previous research shows that the prevalence of problem gambling is higher in young people than in the general adult population.

As in 1997, this study found that commercial gambling games, particularly fruit machines and the National Lottery, are attractive to young people and that a significant minority manage to play them on a regular basis. The proportion of under-16s who spent their money on National Lottery scratchcards in the week prior to the survey has risen significantly since 1997 but this increase was not accompanied by a statistically significant increase in the proportion of illegal sales. The growth in past week expenditure resulted mainly from growth in parental purchases on behalf of their children. Thus Camelot's Project 16 may have had some success in stemming illegal sales in the face of increasing demand.

The study found no significant change since 1997 in the overall prevalence of problem gambling on National Lottery scratchcards among 12-15-year-olds in Britain.

In terms of education, the majority of young people surveyed were aware of the potential risks associated with gambling excessively and the resulting personal and social costs in terms of overspending, addiction and debt. However this did not necessarily dissuade them from playing – even past week players and problem players acknowledged the potential dangers. But evidence from both the 1997 and 1999 surveys suggest less perceived awareness on the part of many parents. The data demonstrate a highly significant link between parental indifference or approval of their children playing the National Lottery under the age of 16 (even to the point of making their purchases for them) and underage participation and problem play.

As in 1997, this study has found a significant association between viewing by under-16s and playing, though this does not necessarily imply a causal link.

The findings from 1997 and this study reveal an active market for commercial gambling among British youth.

- Prepared by Jacinta Ashworth and Nicola Doyle, BMRB Social Research. Part of BMRB International Limited.
- Designed by Dr Sue Fisher, Centre for Research into the Social Impact of Gambling, University of Plymouth.

- The above information is an extract from the National Lottery Commission's web site which can be found at www.natlotcomm.gov.uk

Levy plan to help gambling addicts

Betting companies could be forced to pay to help gambling addicts receive treatment under proposals being considered by Ministers. Sports Minister Richard Caborn is looking at plans to charge the firms a 3 per cent levy to raise up to £3 million a year to help fund treatment programmes for addicts.

The levy, based on turnover, will be introduced if companies prove reluctant to volunteer money for research into the causes and treatment of addiction.

Betting is the fastest growing leisure industry in Britain, according to a recent survey. One in five adults places a bet every week.

The habit has become more socially acceptable since the National Lottery began and is tipped to become more popular after the Government scrapped betting tax last month.

Gambling help groups have seen a huge rise in demands for their services, with Gamblers Anonymous opening one new centre a week. Addicts have access to only one rehabilitation centre in the UK, with just 30 beds. A spokesman for Mr Caborn said last night: 'We are looking at imposing this rate. It would be a way of betting companies helping repair some of the damage that betting can cause.'

Some gaming companies have co-operated with ministerial plans to contribute cash for addicts.

Chris Bell, chief executive of Ladbrokes, the UK's largest bookmaker, has spearheaded plans for a charitable trust to undertake research into problem gambling.

Other companies are less willing to get involved, however.

Paul Bellringer, director of GamCare, the gambling help centre, said last night: 'There is a lot of ambivalence and a lot of reluctance on behalf of some sectors and some companies that the industry should be contributing that sort of figure.'

He said the Government may be forced to introduce a compulsory levy, adding: 'It is going to be very difficult to reach the £3 million target otherwise.'

Getting high on gambling

Information from McGill University

By Sylvain Comeau

The hottest new drug sweeping North American high schools and college campuses has nothing to do with needles, pipes or pills. It's often called an 'invisible addiction', but for a rising number of students, gambling is proving as addictive and destructive as crack cocaine.

Dr Jeffery Derevensky, a professor of educational and counselling psychology, is trying to find out why, and what can be done about it. With a group of graduate students, he is conducting 24 separate studies on youth gambling and his findings so far are alarming.

'Four to eight per cent of adolescents throughout the US and Canada have a serious gambling problem – they are considered pathological gamblers. Another 10 to 15 per cent are at risk of becoming pathological gamblers. The social costs are huge.'

Derevensky has been investigating compulsive gambling for about five years. His research, funded mostly by Loto-Québec since 1994, actually started as a surprising outgrowth of his previous studies of children and game playing.

'One early study we did found that people who play a lot of video games, both male and female, seemed to be gambling much more than people who don't play video games. We believe that there is a transfer of learning and of an illusion of control which is then put on to gambling activities.'

That transfer is inappropriate and dangerous, according to Derevensky. 'When you play a video game, the more you play, the better you get. What looks so random popping up on the screen is really not so random; there are rules built in and that's why people become better as they play.

'These same people are more likely to think that they can also become better players with slot machines or VLTs (video lottery terminals), for example, which is not

the case. But that belief encourages them to gamble again and again.'

According to much of the gambling literature and Derevensky's own studies, most pathological gamblers start playing before the age of 15, many as young as nine or ten. The question is: why are there so many young gamblers now, and why are so many of them out of control?

The first answer is availability.

'This is the first generation to grow up at a time when gambling is so widely available. Going to a bar used to be the common rite of passage; now, for lots of kids, it's going to the casino.' The Montreal Casino opened its doors in 1993, has since expanded twice and is now open 24

> **'Four to eight per cent of adolescents throughout the US and Canada have a serious gambling problem**

hours a day. At the same time, VLTs, popularly known as 'the crack cocaine of gambling', spread into nearly every bar in town.

Derevensky says that adolescents and young adults are at least twice as likely as older adults to become pathological gamblers.

'Adolescents, particularly males, are more attracted to risk-taking activities than adults – you don't see too many adults bungee jumping. As long as gambling is seen by them as an exciting, risk-taking activity, they will be drawn to it.'

But what is the hook that keeps them coming back? At least part of the answer comes from the early days of B.F. Skinner's experiments in behaviourism, according to Rina Gupta, a doctoral student in McGill's applied child psychology programme who is overseeing the gambling studies for Derevensky.

'Early experiments with rats found that they will constantly press a lever if they only occasionally receive a food pellet as a reward psychologists call that intermittent schedules of reinforcement. But the rats who got a food pellet every time they pressed the lever didn't bother pressing it very often because they can get a reward any time.'

Derevensky's team has found that the same psychological mechanism holds true in gambling behaviour.

'Gamblers would be unlikely to maintain their behaviour in the face of constant losses,' Gupta points out, 'but they know that they will win now and then, which incites them to keep playing. With VLTs, for example, many people are more likely to keep playing if it hasn't paid off lately because they think "Okay, it's bound to pay off now."'

In addition to research, Derevensky offers free counselling to a growing number of young gamblers in trouble ('We can't ask them for money because compulsive gamblers never *have* any'), whose ages range from 14 to 21.

David (not his real name), a 19-year-old CEGEP student, sounds like a junkie when he describes the thrill of gambling.

'Nothing in the world matches how I feel when I'm gambling,' he says in a video of an interview with Derevensky. 'Sex doesn't match the high of gambling; I tried weed, and I didn't like it. No, honestly, there's nothing as exciting.'

David, who likes to play high stakes blackjack and roulette at the Montreal Casino, has paid a high price for his thrills. He calculates that he has lost '$100,000 or more', not all of it his own money, since he started gambling. He got the money by begging, borrowing and stealing, and today he is heavily in debt, but still gambling.

'I've lost other people's money. I've borrowed from friends, and paid them back with high interest. I've pawned my possessions thousands of dollars worth of stereo equipment, TV, VCR, camcorder. I've taken large amounts of money from my parents. I've written bad cheques. It's craziness.'

Through counselling, Derevensky tries to help people like David find substitutes for gambling. 'We warn them that they'll probably never find anything quite as exciting as gambling, but they can still develop interests which are an enjoyable alternative.'

He also helps them to form support networks and to address, through psychotherapy, the personal problems which are often caused and aggravated by gambling but which also often encourage them to gamble more.

'Many people gamble to escape their problems. We try to help them confront the problems instead.'

Alarmed at the growing havoc caused by compulsive gambling, Derevensky and his team are going further. Among other initiatives, they are seeking funding to prepare two videos – one aimed at children and the other at adolescents – which would be shown at schools to warn of the dangers of gambling. They have met with social service groups in the US and Canada, to provide training on dealing with gamblers.

'It looks like the number of problem gamblers is going up,' Gupta warns. 'The situation won't improve, and will probably get worse, unless there is a strong campaign in our society for education and prevention. Our message is that gambling is addictive, just like drugs and alcohol.'

'We are not prohibitionists here,' Derevensky insists. 'We are not calling for a ban on gambling. We just want people to be aware that, for a minority, this is a devastating problem.'

• The above information is an extract from the *The McGill Reporter*, the McGill University, Canada's award-winning faculty/staff newspaper. See www.mcgill.ca

Responsible gambling

Information from the Responsible Gambling Council

Problem gambling

Gambling is a problem when it adversely affects: relationships, family, friends; physical, social and mental health; employment; or finances.

Tips for responsible gambling

For many people gambling is exciting and entertaining. They make careful decisions about spending time and money, where to go and how to have fun. The following are some ways people gamble responsibly:
- Gamble for entertainment, not as a way to make money
- Balance gambling with other leisure activities
- Only use discretionary income, not money for everyday expenses

- Set a budget and stick to it
- Don't borrow money to gamble
- Set a time limit
- Take frequent breaks
- Be aware – risk increases at times of loss or depression

Common misconceptions about gambling

Gambling is often regarded with a sense of mystique. Many people believe they can 'win big' over time. The following are some common misconceptions about gambling:
- Gambling is an easy way to make money
- Gambling is the solution to my problems
- I believe I can beat the odds
- Borrowing to gamble is okay

- I can always win it back, I am a lucky person
- This machine is ready for a large payoff
- If you flip a coin and it comes up 'heads' several times in a row, the next time it is more likely to come up 'tails'
- My lottery number is bound to come up if I play it consistently
- I don't have a gambling problem, it's a financial problem
- Gambling is a safe way to escape from my problems

• The above information is an extract from the Responsible Gambling Council's web site which can be found at www.responsiblegambling.org

The hidden addiction

Information from Gamblers Anonymous

Compulsive gambling is an addiction exactly the same as alcoholism or narcotic abuse. It is recognised as a mental illness by the British Medical Association. It does not discriminate; it affects every type of person, be they male or female, young or old, black or white, rich or poor, educated or non-educated. Anybody can be affected by this illness, and many people are. Surveys in Great Britain and America suggest that between $^3/_4$% and 3% of the population are susceptible to this disease. With the population of Great Britain being approximately 60 million people, this suggests that up to 1.8 million people have the potential to have a gambling problem!

GA has no desire to ban gambling in any shape or form, recognising that it is fun for millions upon millions of people. All that GA asks is that the rest of the population, along with government, accepts that certain people have the potential to have a gambling problem and that the more that they are exposed to gambling, the more likely they are to realise this potential for disaster.

Gambling is the hidden addiction. There are no physical signs to identify the victim. If four people walk past you now and return later after indulging in their favourite activity for the last two hours which one is the compulsive gambler? The alcoholic and the narcotic user will both be giving off clues as to having indulged in their favourite pastime, but which of the other two is the compulsive gambler who has just lost every penny in the world and which one has just been doing something normal? The compulsive gambler is very good at hiding their emotions. If you spoke to the compulsive gambler they would appear and act the same as the normal person, although they might ask to borrow a fiver until Monday, because they have left their wallet at home, or got

Written by Patrick, a spokesperson for Gamblers Anonymous

to the bank too late, or not been paid etc., etc.

Being a compulsive gambler makes you a compulsive liar. Having to justify why you have no money makes you very inventive and keeps the brain active. Compulsive gamblers are subject to mood swings. When they are winning they are the most generous, happy-go-lucky people in the world but when they are losing they tend to become irritable and blame everybody else for their problems. If we hadn't argued, I wouldn't have gone down the bookie's and I wouldn't have lost two hundred pounds. No, I don't want to go out. You go out, I'll stay in and get rid of this headache. The important thing now is to find the money for tomorrow's bet. Every penny in the pocket becomes gambling money. That's my stake money. You can't touch that. If a telephone bill comes in for one hundred pounds, and you have two hundred pounds in your pocket, then the normal person pays the bill and has one hundred pounds left to spend as needed. The

compulsive gambler takes the two hundred pounds into the bookie's to win the hundred pounds to pay the phone bill and normally walks out with an unpaid phone bill and no money.

Most compulsive gamblers are good money-getters and when they are not gambling they achieve great things through channelling their efforts into something useful and productive. It could even be argued that they become compulsive about work and even begin to resent spending money. It is as if they have rediscovered the value of money and are trying to make up for the money that they have wasted.

This in essence is one of the secrets of success in escaping from this illness. To stop gambling one has to accept that it has you beaten. You must accept that you have a problem and seek help to overcome it. You must accept that the money that you have lost has gone for ever. I personally said 'God, let me win a thousand pounds and I will never gamble again'. I spent seven thousand pounds trying to win that one thousand pounds. Nobody wants to admit that they are a failure, but in order to beat this disease you must change the way that you think.

You can earn more money but you can never regain the money or the time that you have lost through gambling. To refrain from gambling you must find something else to replace the gambling.

You must plan your time sensibly and avoid leaving time to gamble, and pay particular attention to your usual playtimes. If you always spend Saturdays in the bookie's, then go shopping with the family, watch football with your mates, or plan something different but without leaving the temptation to go for a quick look in the bookie's. You don't go to the barber's unless you want a haircut, so you are not going into the bookie's unless you still want to gamble.

Gambling starts off as a pastime but with some people progresses into a problem. What starts as enjoyment can gradually take over to the point that it becomes the most important thing in life and excludes all other activities. Both work and family activities take a back seat and life comes second to the gambling. The gambler starts lying about their activities and where their money is going. The partner believes the lies because they love the person and have no reason to disbelieve them. Even when it gets to the point that it is Friday night and they wonder why they won't get the money this week! The bank was shut! They didn't pay us! I was mugged on the way home! I lent Bill £50! I paid the deposit on the holiday! The cashpoint ate my card! Eventually it becomes a house of cards and one apparent small problem, be it an 'error' on the bank statement, a credit card statement arriving on the wrong day, leads to the partner discovering the financial truth.

Many partners have admitted relief that it was only gambling. They feared that it was another woman! It was! Lady luck is the worst mistress of them all. Although all addictions are basically the same, Gambling is the one which can take all the money. My money, your money and anybody else's money that I can get hold of, legally or illegally!

A compulsive gambler will end up in one of three places. Prison, the gutter or a box six foot under.

They will have committed a crime to finance their addiction, or lost their home because they did not pay the bills, or have decided that they cannot take the pressure any more. The suicide often happens because of the repeated pattern and the feeling of uselessness . . . I've done it again.

No compulsive gambler ever enters a gambling establishment thinking that they will lose. The feeling of emptiness as they leave the premises is indescribable, but if those feelings could be bottled, then they could earn a fortune. If you were to inhale those feelings of despair every time that you were about to enter the premises, then you would never ever gamble again.

Many people now live productive lives after giving up gambling. A lot of these would not be able to so do without the support of their friends and families

---

The original members of GA were mainly betting shop addicts or casino players. In the last ten years the percentage of fruit machine (one-arm-bandit) players has increased tremendously and the membership also reflects this change in that there are now a large number of under-21s in the fellowship.

The perception of gambling in the community has changed over the last ten years. If you had conducted a survey in the street ten years ago, then most people would have answered along the lines of . . . 'don't talk to me about gambling . . . it's immoral . . . not me I don't gamble'. The same survey today would receive replies like 'It's OK . . . it must be they advertise it on TV'. Gambling is now seen as being socially and morally acceptable and a lot of this is through the advent of the National Lottery. It is still too early to say how many people are becoming compulsive gamblers through the lottery but membership of GA has increased by approximately a third since the introduction of the Lottery and new

meetings are being formed throughout the country.

At the moment if you go to any major town or city in Great Britain then you will find help for alcoholics and narcotic users in the form of drop-in centres or rehab centres. No such help exists for compulsive gamblers. It is time that the government put back resources to help the people with gambling problems.

Many people now live productive lives after giving up gambling. A lot of these would not be able to so do without the support of their friends and families. This shows the great debt that we owe to Gamanon for helping the partners to accept the difficulties of living with a compulsive gambler and showing them how to survive and enable both partners to get well together.

• Gamblers Anonymous (GA) is a self-help group first formed in America in 1957, with the first meetings in Great Britain being held in 1964.

It exists to help anybody who has the desire to stop gambling and runs alongside its sister organisation Gamanon which aims to provide support for friends, family and relatives of the gambler. GA holds meetings in most major towns and cities in Great Britain each week and is self-financing. It avoids contributions from outside agencies since it wishes to remain independent and not be diverted from its main aim. It does not exist for any reason other than to help its members refrain from gambling. Many members of GA have not gambled for many years with some members being 'clean' for over 25 years.

All persons attending GA meetings are guaranteed anonymity. All examples of 'famous' names being mentioned as attending GA meetings have originated from the person themselves.

Gamblers Anonymous can be contacted at PO Box 88, London, SW6 3EU. Tel: 020 7384 3040. E-mail: young.private@gamblersanonymous.org.uk Web site: http://www.gamblersanonymous.org.uk

ADDITIONAL RESOURCES

You might like to contact the following organisations for further information. Due to the increasing cost of postage, many organisations cannot respond to enquiries unless they receive a stamped, addressed envelope.

Addiction Recovery Foundation
Addiction Today
122a Wilton Road
London
SW1V 1JZ
Tel: 020 7233 5333
Fax: 020 7233 8123
E-mail:
enquiries@addictiontoday.co.uk
Web site: Web site:
www.addictiontoday.co.uk
Addiction Today publishes the most influential information in the UK on addiction recovery. In fact, it is the ONLY magazine in the UK devoted to recovery from addiction. See their web site for subscription details.

Gamblers Anonymous and Gamanon
PO Box 88
London
SW6 3EU
Tel: 020 7384 3040
E-mail:
young.private@gamblersanonymous.org.uk
Web site:
www.gamblersanonymous.org.uk
Gamblers Anonymous is a self-help fellowship of men and women who have joined together to do something about their gambling problem. See their web site for a list of their helpline numbers.

GamCare
Catherine House
25-27 Catherine Place
London
SW1E 6DU
Tel: 020 7233 8988
Fax: 020 7233 8977
E-mail: director@gamcare.org.uk
Web site: www.gamcare.org.uk
GamCare is gambling neutral. The charity does not wish to restrict the choices or opportunities for anyone to operate, or engage in, gambling opportunities that are legally available in the UK. GamCare has a commitment to promote responsible attitudes to gambling and to work for the provision of proper care for those who have been harmed by a gambling dependency. Runs a helpline 0845 6000 133 –10 am to 10 pm. Monday to Friday.

National Centre for Social Research
35 Northampton Square
London
EC1V 0AX
Tel: 020 7250 1866
Fax: 020 7250 1524
E-mail: info@natcen.ac.uk
Web site: www.natcen.ac.uk
The National Centre is the largest independent social research institute in Britain. It conducts social research among members of the public to provide information on a range of social policy issues in Britain.

National Lottery Commission
2 Monck Street
London
SW1P 2BQ
Tel: 020 7227 2000
Fax: 020 7227 2015
E-mail:
national.lottery@btinternet.com
Web site: www.natlotcomm.gov.uk
The National Lottery Commission is a new non-departmental public body, which began on the 1 April 1999 to regulate the National Lottery, a task formerly carried out by the Office of the National Lottery (OFLOT). The Commission undertakes the statutory duties set down in the National Lottery Act 1993, which previously lay with the Director General of the National Lottery. These are to ensure that the National Lottery is run with all due propriety and that the interests of participants are protected; and, subject to these two considerations, to maximise the amounts of money raised for the Good Causes. For information about how the National Lottery is run, draw results, queries and complaints, contact Camelot: 0845 910 0000 (local call rate).

Responsible Gambling Council (Ontario)
505 Consumers Road
Suite 801
Toronto
Ontario
CANADA
M2J 4V8
Tel: + 1 416 499 9800
Fax: + 1 416 499 8260
E-mail: infosource@rgco.org
Web site:
www.responsiblegambling.org
The Responsible Gambling Council (Ontario) is committed to ensuring healthy individuals, families and communities that are free of the personal, social and economic harm resulting from gambling abuse.

INDEX

age
  and participation in gambling 8
  restrictions on gambling 2, 27
    and illegal sales 34-5
    under 16s understanding of 35-6
behaviourism, and compulsive gambling 37-8
betting
  age restrictions on 27
  online 12, 13, 14-15
  private bets 7, 8
  and problem gamblers 35
  systems 28
betting shops 3, 40
  lifting of restrictions on 1, 22
bingo 2, 3, 7, 8, 9, 22
  age restrictions 18, 27
  expenditure on 8, 9
Blackpool, Las Vegas-style gambling at 2, 16, 17, 18, 23
bookmaker bets 7, 9
  online 12
  and problem gamblers 9
  see also betting shops; dog racing; horse racing
bookmakers, contributions to assist compulsive gamblers
    36
boys, and expenditure on the National Lottery 35

casinos
  age restrictions 18, 27
  Las Vegas-style in Britain 2, 16, 17
  lifting of restrictions on 1, 2, 16, 17, 22
    effects of 2
  Montreal 37, 38
  odds on winning casino games 28
  online 10-11, 12, 13
  percentage of the population visiting 7
  and problem gamblers 9
  and social class 8
children, and compulsive gambling 19, 25
cognitive behaviour techniques, overcoming compulsive
gambling with 29-30
compulsive gambling 18-40
  abstinence or control 30, 31
  advice on controlling 20, 39-40
  asking questions about 25, 30, 31-3
  and betting games 35
  British Gambling Prevalence Survey on 9
  and children 19, 25
  company levies to pay for treatment 36
  consequences of 27-8
  defining 31, 39
  dream world of the compulsive gambler 33
  families and what to do 28
  and fruit machines 35, 36
  and Gamblers Anonymous 15, 18, 19, 25, 26, 31-3
  and the National Lottery 9, 19, 21, 26
    and under 16s 34-6

online 14, 19
overcoming 29-30
periodic 32
personal experiences of 22
and personality traits 32-3, 39
prevalence of 1-2
profile of problem gamblers 9
reasons for addiction 27
relapse-prevention strategy 30
signs and symptoms of 24-5, 27, 29-30
and television 19
and UK gambling law reforms 16, 17, 18-19, 22-3
in the United States 37-8
and willpower 31-2
and young people 2, 19, 37-8
criminals, and gambling 1, 17, 22

dog racing 2, 8, 9

families, of compulsive gamblers 28
football pools
  age restrictions 18, 27
  expenditure on 9
  and men 8, 9
  and the National Lottery 3
  online 12
  percentage of the population participating 7
fruit machines
  age restrictions 2
  expenditure on 9
  and men 8
  percentage of people playing 7
  and problem gamblers 35, 36, 40
  proposed bans on 1

Gamblers Anonymous 15, 19, 26, 36, 39-40
  in America 18, 25
  and Gamanon 40
  questions listed by 30
  Recovery Programme 32
  and spirituality 33
gambling
  amount of money placed on a bet 3
  bingo 2, 3, 7, 8, 9, 18, 22, 27
  bookmaker bets 7, 9, 12
  common misconceptions about 38
  dog racing 2, 8, 9
  expenditure on 8-9, 17
  football pools 3, 7, 8, 9, 12, 18, 27
  fruit machines 1, 2, 7, 8, 9, 35, 36, 40
  horse racing 2, 3, 7, 8, 9, 19
  international comparisons 1-2, 7, 9
  on the Internet see Internet, online gambling
  keeping it under control 2
  libertarian arguments for 23
  minimal interest gamblers 8, 9
  moderate interest gamblers 8

multiple interest gamblers 8, 9
odds of winning 2
participation in
   and age 8
   in Britain 7-9
   and gender 3, 8
   percentage of the population 3, 7
   and social class 3, 8, 13
percentage of non-gamblers 7-8
profits of the gambling industry 2
reasons for present law 1
responsible 38
social impact of deregulated 1
and social relationships 32
spread-betting 7
UK law on
   liberalisation 1, 16, 17, 18-19, 22-3
   online gambling 12
and women 3, 8, 9, 26
and young people 2, 37-8
see also casinos; compulsive gambling; National Lottery
GamCare 1, 2, 14, 20, 21
   on company levies for helping compulsive gamblers 36
   on controlling your gambling 20
gender, and participation in gambling 3, 8, 9
girls, and expenditure on the National Lottery 35
Government policies
   on gambling
      betting taxes 2, 17, 23, 36
      company levies for treating compulsive gamblers 36
      liberalisation of the law on 1, 16, 17, 18-19, 22-3
      online gambling 12

horse racing
   age restrictions on gambling 2
   expenditure on 9
   future of 19
   and interactive television 19
   and men 8
   percentage of people participating 7
   and women 3

incomes, gambling and income levels 3, 8
Internet
   online gambling 3, 4, 7, 10-15, 23
      in America 25
      betting 12
      casinos 10-11, 13
      characteristics of users 12-13
      and children 25
      estimated turnover 13-14
      gaming 11
      number of users 13
      regulation of 12
      and revenue losses to the Treasury 16

lotteries
   online 12
   see also National Lottery

men
   and compulsive gambling 26
   and gambling 8

betting shops 3
   expenditure on 9
National Lottery
   age restrictions 2, 4, 27
      under 16s understanding of 35-6
   and Camelot Group plc 4, 5, 6, 19, 21, 34-5
   distributing organisations 5
   and the image of gambling 19
   InstantsTM 4, 6, 21, 35
   integrity of the draw 5
   odds of winning 2
   online 12, 21
   players
      expenditure 8, 9, 35
      percentage of the population 3, 4, 7, 8
   prize money
      target shortfall 6
      value of in each game 6
   and problem gamblers 9, 19, 21, 26
      under 16s 34-6
   promoter's licence 4
   restriction of to the UK 4
   retailers 4
   social impact 1, 40
   stakeholders 6
   and television 19, 35
   and women 3
   and young people 21, 26, 34-6
   see also scratch cards

parents, and children playing the National Lottery 36
pools *see* football pools

roulette, odds of winning 2

scratch cards
   age restrictions 27
   expenditure on 9
   odds of winning 2
   percentage of the population buying 7, 8
   and problem gamblers 9, 26
      under 16s 34, 35, 36
slot machines
   age and the law 27
   odds of winning 2
social class, and gambling 3, 8, 13
spread-betting 7

taxes, gambling 2, 17, 23, 36
television
   interactive, and online gambling 12, 13, 14-15, 19, 23
   and the National Lottery 19, 35
television programmes, Jackpot 3

video games, and compulsive gambling 37

women
   and gambling 3, 8
      compulsive 26
      expenditure on 9

young people
   and compulsive gambling 2, 19, 37-8
   and the National Lottery 21, 26, 34-6

ACKNOWLEDGEMENTS

The publisher is grateful for permission to reproduce the following material.

While every care has been taken to trace and acknowledge copyright, the publisher tenders its apology for any accidental infringement or where copyright has proved untraceable. The publisher would be pleased to come to a suitable arrangement in any such case with the rightful owner.

Chapter One: Current Trends

Gambling, © Guardian Newspapers Limited 2001, *A safe bet?*, © GamCare, *Lottery gives women a taste for gambling*, © The Daily Mail, August 2001, *Lottery guide*, © National Lottery Commission, *Weekly average expenditure by household*, © National Lottery Commission, *Where does the money go?*, © National Lottery Commission, *Lottery money*, © National Lottery Commission, *Gambling behaviour in Britain*, © National Centre for Social Research/GamCare, *Lottery good causes that go off course*, © Telegraph Group Limited, London 2001, *Primary mode of client gambling by age*, © GamCare, *Chips with everything*, © Amy Vickers, *Attitudes towards internet betting*, © BMRB/Mintel April 2001, Guardian Newspapers Limited 2001, *On-line gambling*, © Crown copyright is reproduced with the permission of the Controller of Her Majesty's Stationery Office, *Take a gamble on digital betting*, © Richard Kilgarriff, *Play-as-you-view*, © Guardian Newspapers Limited 2001, *Blackpool to be Las Vegas-on-sea*, © Telegraph Group Limited, London 2001, *Mega-casinos on UK horizon*, © Guardian Newspapers Limited 2001.

Chapter Two: Compulsive Gambling

So gambling is safe. You want to bet?, © Cristina Odone, *Britain rolled over by lure of the lottery*, © Telegraph Group Limited, London 2001, *A sure bet?*, © GamCare, *Gambling by gender*, © GamCare, *Excessive participation*, © National Lottery Commission, *Gambling does destroy lives*, © Roy Hattersley, *Confessions of an online gambler*, © Guardian Newspapers Limited 2001, *Signs, symptoms and stresses*, © GamCare, *Primary mode of client gambling*, © GamCare, *Would you believe a problem gambler aged 8?*, © iafrica.com, *GA and compulsive gambling*, © Gamblers Anonymous, *Supporting a problem gambler*, © GamCare 2001, *So gambling is all about luck? Wrong!*, © iafrica.com, *Overcoming compulsive gambling*, © Addiction Today, *Gambling FAQs*, © Gamblers Anonymous, *Under -6s and the National Lottery*, © National Lottery Commission, *Levy plan to help gambling addicts*, © The Daily Mail, October 2001, *Getting high on gambling*, © The McGill Reporter, *Responsible gambling*, © The Responsible Gambling Council – Ontario, *The hidden addiction*, © Gamblers Anonymous.

Photographs and illustrations:

Pages 1, 22, 26, 34, 39: Pumpkin House, pages 2, 12, 17, 21, 27, 29, 31, 37: Simon Kneebone.

Craig Donnellan
Cambridge
January, 2002